Praise for *Frog Mountain Blues*

"[Bowden] catches the attractiveness, ambiguity, artificiality, and frightening developmental pace of urbanizing Arizona with a fine-tuned eye and ear, and lays out bluntly what is at stake. . . . He has written an engaging, thoughtful, and tough-minded book."
—*WESTERN AMERICAN LITERATURE*

"A microcosm . . . of the 'civilized' overuse of the entire planet."
—*BLOOMSBURY REVIEW*

"Anyone interested in the survival of our most precious natural places should read this book."
—BRUCE BABBITT, FORMER SECRETARY OF THE INTERIOR

"Stunning photography by Pulitzer Prize–winning photographer Jack W. Dykinga lends a vivid visual dimension to Bowden's message. . . . Dykinga's evocative photography and Bowden's relentless pen render the human erosion of the Santa Catalina Mountains painfully clear and give *Frog Mountain Blues* an undeniably strong emotional impact."
—*ECOLOGY LAW QUARTERLY*

"An elegiac, ecology-minded tribute to Tucson's Santa Catalina Mountains. . . . A handsome book with elegant graphics and astounding photos."

—*KIRKUS REVIEWS*

"Here's the new American nature writing—resourceful, funny, personal, full of good facts, words of the locals, hard-hitting but not self-righteous . . . a case history of how America destroys itself."

—GARY SNYDER

"A lively and informative meditation on the maddening, absurd, but still somehow hopeful relationship between an exploding western megalopolis and the still somehow wild mountain range that overlooks it."

—DAVID RAINS WALLACE

"A moving, passionate eulogy for a place that, if not altogether dead, has been ravaged and mutilated, even by those who professed to love it."

—DONALD WORSTER

FROG MOUNTAIN BLUES

FROG MOUNTAIN BLUES

CHARLES BOWDEN

PHOTOGRAPHS BY JACK W. DYKINGA

FOREWORD BY ALISON HAWTHORNE DEMING

THE UNIVERSITY OF
ARIZONA PRESS

TUCSON

The University of Arizona Press
www.uapress.arizona.edu

Copyright © 1987, 1994, 2018 by The Arizona Board of Regents
All rights reserved.
New foreword published 2018

ISBN-13: 978-0-8165-3792-1 (paper)

Cover design by Leigh McDonald
Cover photo by Keith Marroquin

Library of Congress Cataloging-in-Publication Data
Names: Bowden, Charles, 1945–2014, author. | Dykinga, Jack W., photographer. | Deming,
    Alison Hawthorne, 1946– writer of foreword.
Title: Frog Mountain blues / Charles Bowden ; photographs by Jack W. Dykinga ; foreword
    by Alison Hawthorne Deming.
Description: Tucson : The University of Arizona Press, 2018. | Originally published in 1987.
    | Includes bibliographical references.
Identifiers: LCCN 2018014802 | ISBN 9780816537921 (pbk. : alk. paper)
Subjects: LCSH: Natural history—Arizona—Santa Catalina Mountains. | Nature conser-
    vation—Arizona—Santa Catalina Mountains. | Human ecology—Arizona—Santa
    Catalina Mountains. | Santa Catalina Mountains (Ariz.)—Description and travel.
Classification: LCC QH105.A4 B69 2018 | DDC 508.791/75—dc23 LC record available at
    https://lccn.loc.gov/2018014802

Printed in the United States of America
♾ This paper meets the requirements of ANSI/NISO Z39.48–1992 (Permanence of Paper).

For my mother, Berdina Beermann Bowden,
who taught me love is always the answer.

Tucson and the Santa Catalina Mountains

*The old Papago sits his brown hand curled around the
Coors Tall Boy. His dead legs hang off the wheel chair,
and he wants a shaman fetched from the hot desert to
the west. He looks past the broken truck in the yard and
beyond the fields to the line where the city rises up and
gnaws the earth into asphalt and straight streets.
The eyes are going and he peers through thick lenses
at the Santa Catalina Mountains which tower over the
smog and buildings like a maimed stone god. I ask the
name of the highest peak in the tongue of his people.
"Frog Mountain," he replies.
There is no further explanation and his silence flat-
tens the air. But I know and the beer cannot confuse me.
Frog Mountain has got the blues.*

CONTENTS

FOREWORD

Charles Bowden is an essential writer of the American Southwest. He was driven by a hunger for wild places and wild life that took him into the mountains and into the darker recesses of urban life. Born in Chicago, he first came to Tucson as a boy when his family moved from the Windy City to the desert. Years earlier, his father had tossed him a copy of Walter Noble Burns's *Tombstone*, and, parsing his way through the words as he lay on the rug of their Chicago home, he began to stoke his appetite for the mythic West. He found out

about wild men that followed burros into the Apache Hills and searched for a heart of gold or silver. They settled their arguments with guns and answered to no person or government, and when they finally struck it rich the money proved somehow not enough and so they always headed back into the hills, leading another burro toward an El Dorado called freedom and big sky.

"Parse." That is Bowden's word for how, as a child, he found his way into the world through attending to words. It is an apt one for the man he would become, a man with such a keen ear for the rhythms of American language, the cadence of a sentence, an eye for the muscular verb or metaphor, that his writing woos into its embrace even a feminist such as myself who is dismissive of the hypermasculine fantasy of the Old West. Bowden may have looked and dressed like a Marlboro man, a rocky crag of a man with a voice deep as granite, but he was more complex and learned than that stereotype, more driven by a passion for telling difficult truths, more certain that bearing witness to his time and place mattered than any cardboard cutout of a man.

At sixteen, he got a job helping an ecological survey of the Santa Catalinas that furthered his apprenticeship to the mountain. He lived in Summerhaven, spending days hiking section after section of the range, marking out sampling sites for a census of plant population, and nights studying botany books. He attended the University of Arizona and the University of Wisconsin, where he worked on a PhD in American intellectual history. He walked out during his dissertation defense, offended by the questions he was asked. It is easy to see Bowden making such a move. He had little tolerance for pretension or obfuscation. He was not really fit for academic life, more at home on a backcountry hike or birdwatching or wrestling with the language until it sounded more like a barroom conversation than an academic dissertation. Let's say he had a supremely well-tempered bullshit detector.

His chops as a writer were formed during a three-year stint as a reporter for the *Tucson Citizen,* during which he stumbled into a beat reporting on violence against women and children, a nightmarish pursuit that led him into the dark alleys of his own psyche. Years later he wrote the essay "Torch Song" for *Harper's Magazine,* one of his most widely read and anthologized pieces, reflecting on the experience and its troubling personal ramifications. It was a hard plane of intensity in which he had worked, and so to calm himself, he wrote a book about a mountain titled *Frog Mountain Blues*. But Charles Bowden, it seems, could never be calm. He describes himself in the book as educated in the school of "Tom Paine and the Whisky Rebellion," a man "out of step with the basic drives of my nation." He turns to the old ways in naming the place. Frog Mountain, the Tohono O'odham name for the summit of Tucson's Catalinas, becomes the central character of the book, the beleaguered hero, "a force that could stop a city in its tracks," "the wild ground that questions the way we live." And for Bowden, Frog Mountain in this fine and cantankerous book has the blues.

Bowden argues against the idea that perpetual growth and its "ongoing orgy of consumption" means progress, proposing that the paved roads up the mountain be blown up and the mountain left alone to heal. The only way to protect the mountain, he writes, is to leave it alone, to let the mountain "seek out its own ends." He always wanted to write about nature, the ground on which he stood and hiked. In doing so, he ran headlong into the forces that would diminish what he loved: a landscape "being buried by housing" and, to his self-skeptical eye, "the economic machine that feeds me." It is a winning position to take when writing about nature. He claims no self-righteous stance in arguing to save the mountain. He speaks as complicit, as a cog in the machine of our age. Neither the backpacker nor the cowman can claim a moral high ground in leaving the mountain to its own devices. When Bowden sits in a bar swapping mountain talk over beers with a man who has spent his life working for the U.S. Geological Survey, he cops to the ironies of their "big plans for the mountain." "We are sinners," he writes, "considering virtue, yet relishing our memories of past sins."

Frog Mountain Blues sets the trajectory for Bowden's future work. I first read the book early in the 1990s, when I was new to the Southwest. I was immediately won over by Bowden's gorgeous prose, his exactitude and music, and his argument that the reason to protect the place has more to do with love than with

---

conservation, ecology, wilderness areas, national parks, endangered species, diversity, ecosystem, biome, biosphere. I approve. Yes, yes. I'll sign your petition, write the congressman maybe, join the organization.

But these matters are a kind of polite conversation in a clean, well-appointed room. The chairs are comfortable but the air lacks scent and things feel dull to the touch. These things do not move me and do not bring me to the mountain.

Journalism taught Bowden to look outward for his subject matter. But some fiery energy in his soul taught him to write with irrepressible passion. In *Frog Mountain Blues* he sees beauty where others see an opportunity for profit and wealth. And he lauds others who see beauty, like Buster Bailey, the old Pusch Ridge cowman profiled in the book, who hates seeing cattle land being surrounded by "these goddam backpackers." Bailey reflects, "That old mountain . . . that's been the beauty thing of my life." By the time Bowden wrote this book, he was no longer the hothead who leaves the room when he doesn't like the questions. He was the man who stayed in the room when the hard questions needed to be asked. And he listened. He took seriously the obligation to be a witness and historian. Rather than getting stuck in lament at the failure to protect the mountain as he had envisioned when he first wrote the book, he moved on to expose the forces of destruction and diminishment.

The last decade of Bowden's prolific writing life was devoted to documenting systems of corruption and greed—the savings-and-loan scandal and the brutal violence troubling the Southwest borderlands. He became friends with many of his interview subjects, individuals with whom he would have had deep philosophical and moral disagreement, most notably Charles Keating, the Arizona developer who was convicted of fraud and racketeering, and El Sicario, the contract killer working for Mexican drug lords who, at the end of his career, found both Jesus and a contract out on his head. Bowden went places as a writer that few would dare and sought truths few would tell. In an interview he said, "I didn't want to be the reporter who discovers the Jews are getting killed in 1945. I wanted to be the guy who reported it in 1939." As an uncompromising voice for truth, a researcher with balls of steel, and a writer of lyrical force, he remains indispensable in showing us the darker aspects of what we are as a culture, with all of our grievous flaws. And he still could celebrate what he loved.

Are there elements to his writing that feel dated at the time of this reissue coming thirty years after its original publication? Certainly there are. The degree to which climate change has intensified concern for the land and its creatures, yoking these issues with concerns for social justice, is missing. But that is a factor of historical perspective that has become apparent only as climate change science has given compelling evidence of the linkages between environmental and cultural degradation. Bowden is not at his best writing about Native cultures of the region, and his portrayals of women, if not absent, are nearly always painfully inflected toward stilettos and fishnets (though this book spares the reader those diminishments). *Frog Mountain Blues* honors the O'odham by calling forth their traditional name for the mountain, but his depiction of the contemporary O'odham culture seems ruefully dismissive and lacking in empathy. How would he have met our moment of hyperacute sensitivity to cultural misrepresentation? I wish he were still here to say. We could use his fire and insistence on evidence-based thinking now.

Bowden claimed early in *Frog Mountain Blues* that he could not follow Leopold's dictum to think like a mountain, but by the time he moves through documenting in this book his experiences and those of others who have found meaning in the mountain, he finds the capacity to feel his way into the mountain's aggrieved condition. It becomes a patient, wounded and faltering from assault.

With each passing day, your strength dwindles but your attendants do not seem alarmed by this fact. Your chart does not say critical or stable or chronic, but simply, "Land of Many Uses."

I think the doctors should consider some new medicine if we wish for the patient to survive our care.

Frog Mountain Blues continues to be an important book for learning to read this place through the eyes of experience and history, and Bowden remains a sobering voice for facing our failures in protecting what we love in this time of global destruction, for taking seriously the power of language to set ourselves right again with the enormous task of living with purpose and presence and care on the land.

Alison Hawthorne Deming, 2018

FROG MOUNTAIN BLUES

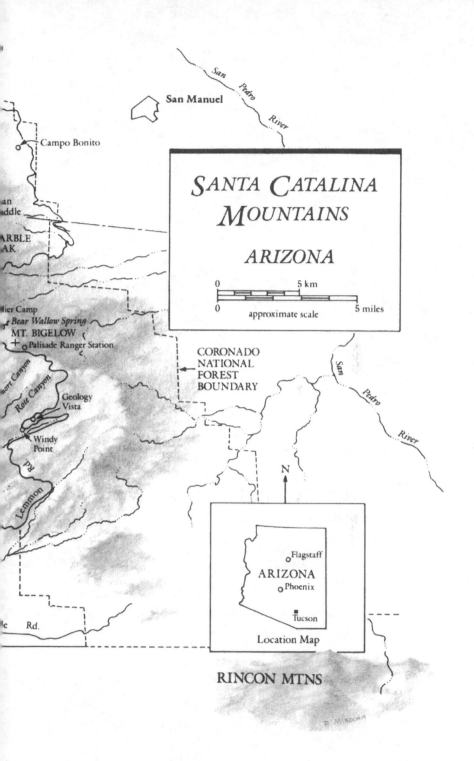

San Manuel

San
Pedro

River

Campo Bonito

an
iddle

ARBLE
AK

ier Camp
Bear Wallow Spring
MT. BIGELOW
Palisade Ranger Station

hore Canyon

Rose Canyon

Geology
Vista

Windy
Point

Rd.

Lemmon

Rd.

SANTA CATALINA MOUNTAINS

ARIZONA

0	5 km
0	approximate scale	5 miles

CORONADO
NATIONAL
FOREST
BOUNDARY

San

Pedro

River

N

ARIZONA

Flagstaff

Phoenix

Tucson

Location Map

RINCON MTNS

P. MIROCHA

LAST CALL

Santa Catalina Mountains

El. 8000–9000   *Loc.: Pima Co., Arizona*

In 1697, Fr. Kino visited a now vanished Papago ranche-ria near what is today Tucson and called the place Santa Catalina Cuitchibaque. It was here in 1756 that Fr. Ber-nard Middendorf attempted unsuccessfully to establish a mission, being dissuaded from this because of the cruelty of the Indians. The name Santa Catalina, or Catarina, was applied by Fr. Kino to the mountains bordering the valley to the north and east. Since it was customary for missionaries to name localities for the saint's day on which such places were first visited, it may well be that Fr. Kino gave these mountains their name on the same day (St. Catherine's day) on which he christened the Indian village nearby.

BYRD H. GRANGER, WILL C. BARNES'S
ARIZONA PLACE NAMES

We talk idly. The smooth oak table feels solid to the touch. The room offers warm pastel walls and soft light. The bar heads toward closing time and we sit over our drinks in an island of urban peace.

The man has spent his life in Tucson, worked for years with the U.S. Geological Survey, devoted hundreds of hours to plundering the historical archives. He used to hunt and for him the ground is a mishmash of hard science, old historical accounts, and the feel of a fall day as he sighted on a deer. He is an individual seemingly embedded in facts and dedicated to reason; normally when he speaks his words are both quick and measured.

"What about the mountain?" I ask. "What should be done with the range? What would you do if there were no holds barred?"

He hesitates and fingers the rim of his glass of beer and then he begins an inventory of his youth and the Catalinas. He remembers when the paved highway went up the south side of the mountain in 1950 and how wonderful it was suddenly to be able to drive from the desert floor to the pines in an hour. He starts ticking off teenage hijinks—night rides, drunken parties, things that come booming back into his mind when he thinks of the Santa Catalinas.

His stories trigger my own inventory and suddenly I am sitting in this peaceful bar recalling being sixteen years old in Sabino Canyon, the major cut in the mountain's south face, and perching on a big rock by the stream at night, pitching empty beer bottles against the boulders, and watching the glass shards go tumbling into the roaring white water.

So we sit over beers with our memories and feel a little odd about setting big plans for the mountain and creating wish lists of changes. We are sinners considering virtue, yet relishing our memories of past sins.

But after a moment, the man warms to the task. Let's start at the top, he smiles, and consider the observatories for astronomy and infrared research, the ski lodge, and the radio towers. Are the scientists worth the sacrifice of the peaks? Can police communications

and popular music justify the destruction of the crest? And is it
sensible to cut big swaths of timber down for ski runs on a mountain sixty miles from Mexico that at best offers only sometime powder for the sport?

"You know," he says. "There is no Bill of Rights for mountain
tops."

Then he drops down to Summerhaven, the cluster of hundreds
of cabins perched on the mountain, a community that for years has
spilled sewage into the streams. Why not remove them and all the
other pockets of cabins, he wonders, and leave the top as a natural area? He questions the picnic grounds with their pavementlike
appearance of stomped earth from the pounding of human feet
gathered around tables and barbecue pits.

He smiles broadly now, as if aware he has drifted into a state of
pure fantasy. He is living in the Sunbelt where people keep moving
in and mountains keep shrinking from their touch and there seems
no sense in the ideas he is offering. All over the West the land is in
retreat. Why bother to talk about anything but growth and development and bulldozer blades slicing the earth?

But he cannot resist. Take out the road, he says, close it or blow
it up, whatever it takes for the mountain to become a place you visit
on foot or not at all.

Outside the quiet bar, a slow winter rain falls over Tucson, and
within the soft gauze of clouds and cool droplets the mountain
sleeps. Over a few beers, this rockpile is an abstraction, a topic
like professional football or foreign policy. But this subject really
exists. We know it. We have touched it, walked it, felt it rub against
our lives.

Without the Santa Catalina Mountains, Tucson is just another
city in a nation of urban islands. The range is the heart and soul of
this community, but for decades the city has sold the mountain as
it clawed its way toward the magical goals of growth and wealth.
The stone skyline exists in every car sold, every house slammed

Windy Point

against the desert floor, and every steak sizzled over a mesquite fire in a cowboy restaurant. The ridges rest on the faces of people prowling the malls and wash across the bodies of thousands stalled in the daily traffic jams of the rush. We do not know who we are until we look at the mountain. We have not been able to resist our hunger for the huge stone wall that frames our lives. We plug the canyons with resorts, put our observatories on the peaks, and creep up its slopes with dream homes nibbling at the National Forest boundaries.

Sometimes we pause and regret these acts. But we cannot seem to stop and we always go back and take yet more.

This is the constant story of the West, the region that people pour into seeking some bleary eyed vision of freedom, the region we all want to possess and then seem to maim with our endless appetites. The gnashing teeth of our hungers have chewed their way across this continent, and now the mountains—all the mountains lording it over all the cities, all the wild ground our ancestors called tractless wastes—now these spots are our last memories of a better world where the landscape once hammered us into a new kind of people. All the words and catch phrases we pray live in our bones— Never Give An Inch, Self-Reliance, Waste Not Want Not, Every Man For Himself, No Free Lunch, Suck In Your Gut We're Goin' to Whup It!—all our boasts and sweet dreams of freedom beckon from the rough slopes and still promise to nurture us.

I was having a beer with Dave Brown, a game biologist who has spent a lot of time searching the West for glimpses of the wild— grizzlies, wolves, bighorn sheep, antelope, elk—and we started talking about where we had been most alone.

He said without even thinking, "A canyon in the Santa Catalina Mountains on the back side. I'd been collecting squirrels and I was supposed to meet a guy at some junction of this canyon with a side gulch and I get there first and night falls. I make a fire and I'm standing around in the glow of the blaze like a cave man and there's something about that country. I didn't even see planes flying overhead that day, and I'm huddled there over this fire and I felt alone, so alone."

He just sat there sipping his drink and smiling at the memory of being left to himself while a Sunbelt city of half a million roared just over the crest.

When I was a kid in Chicago—I must have been eight or nine—my father came home one day from his stint in the Loop and tossed me a paperback copy of Walter Noble Burns's *Tombstone* and that was my introduction to this place called the West. It was winter and the light failed early. I stretched out on the rug by my mother's treadle sewing machine and parsed my way through the words and found out about wild men that followed burros into the Apache Hills and searched for a heart of gold or silver. They settled their arguments with guns and answered to no person or government, and when they finally struck it rich the money proved somehow not enough and so they always headed back into the hills, leading another burro toward an El Dorado called freedom and big sky.

Years later when I grew up, I learned that Walter Noble Burns was considered a newspaper hack who spun yarns, but this new information never touched the memory of that initial reading or tempered my belief. I got my first whiff of freedom in that little paperback book, and I never gave up trailing that scent.

All over the West, there are remnants of that time, places that still offer the Big Lonely and days without walls. We try to talk about these matters, but the words always come out as categories like National Parks or National Monuments or National Forests or Wilderness Areas. Or sometimes as summer cabins, ski lodges, and resorts.

The Santa Catalinas are just one of these ancient pockets and to look deep into their stone walls is to catch a glimpse of what is possible for ourselves as a people and what must not be surrendered.

There is a distance that must be crossed from the safe country where we now live to this other world, a place that at first looks hostile to us. That journey takes us to the wild ground that tugs at our memory and spooks us with its power.

I start at first light and bicycle up the mountain before the heat of day. Cars slow down briefly and the drivers stare at me and roar past. The big views flow over my handlebars at eight miles an hour. At the picnic grounds I see people eating and enjoying themselves. At the mountain cabins I sense the city ebbing from the bodies of weekend vacationers. The ski lodge promises cold beer, chair lifts, and winter dreams of white powder. When I finally pedal to the summit, I think the big peak belongs to me, and the place becomes a haven of sweat, ache, and quiet.

Just as I climb off the bike, a man of sixty trots up a mountain trail finishing a nineteen-mile run from the desert floor. My mountain falls away under the power of his.

He has found something out on the slopes I had not dreamed of, and now I want it also. And there are whole worlds out there he has not touched. The thing does not end but goes deeper and deeper just so long as we let it exist.

I need these places. I am a child sprawled on the floor in a Chicago apartment, and a paperback book feeds the message of the West into my hungry mind. I am in my thirties and I hike 150 miles across an uninhabited desert. I am a man sitting in a bar with friends and talking about what the mountain means and what must be done to save the mountain from ourselves so that we can keep it forever.

When I say these words to other people, the thoughts are usually dismissed. The mountains and the wild ground are acknowledged to be fine places and my notions are all well and good, but there is this unmistakable feeling in the air that I am being excessive, that I am going too far, that I am being unreasonable. People give me a kind of shrug as if I were entitled to my hobby, just as they are

Bigelow Road

entitled to their favorite ways of killing time. Somehow in their eyes the wild ground is a thing like bowling—a reasonable activity if you're interested in that kind of thing.

I cannot abide this reaction. Perhaps it is logical for some people to consider our cities and the Santa Catalinas equivalent things, simply a matter of personal preference. But it is also madness. We have enough mill towns, boom towns, strip cities, and concrete plains of subdivisions, and if we want more, we can easily build them. We have never built a range like the Santa Catalinas, and there is no surplus of such ground in our world.

Of course, these arguments seldom occur. There is no point in pushing such matters. No one is convinced; no one shifts positions. Instead, I usually do something quite different.

I shoulder a pack and start walking and looking for those things that are hard to name but easy to feel. And I know where to go. I go to the deserts, the forests, the plains, and the peaks. I go to the mountain.

Backside road sign

HEART OF GOLD

---

*We drove on to Tucson. Tucson is situated in beauti-
ful mesquite riverbed country, overlooked by the snowy
Catalina range. The city was one big construction job; the
people transient, wild, ambitious, gay; washlines, trailers;
bustling downtown with banners; altogether very California. Fort Lowell Road . . . wound along lovely riverbed
trees in the flat desert.*

JACK KEROUAC, *ON THE ROAD*, 1957

*The town of Tucson became mad with the news when
it was spread around and prospectors rushed to locate
claims in the Catalinas but failed to find the place mentioned by the two prospectors.*

*From 1880 on, numerous attempts have been made
to solve the mystery of the old Spanish mine, The Mine
with the Iron Door, and to relocate the ancient Nueva Mia
Ciudad, Nine Mile City of legend. No one has ever gained
wealth in the Cañada del Oro district, although placer
mining to this day yields a day's wages.*

ARIZONA DAILY STAR, AUGUST 3, 1927

The sky hangs dark like the lid on a Dutch oven and the colors soften in the weak rays of the sun. Pale green lichen licks across the gray boulder and I sit and stare at the ground near my feet. I make an inventory like a factory owner trying to grasp just what he has in stock. I am not trained in the natural sciences, and I always seem to begin my wanderings with little surveys as if some kind of listing will make sense out of the clutter of life that surrounds me.

Twigs from oak, sycamore, and ash lace the forest floor, tree bones of steel gray, gunmetal blue, and black. Leaves mat underfoot with sharp angles and gentle curves: brown leaves, russet leaves, tan, beige, black, gray, pale green, dark brown, silver. Six inches from my right boot, new shoots caress the decay with blue-green tendrils.

That is one square foot in the Cañada del Oro, the big canyon that knifes the back side of the Santa Catalinas. The overhead clouds roll tighter and pack into a wall of darkness. The forest here is rinsed of brilliance, with only a rare daub of red from the sumac, not one slash of yellow. This has the feel of the Wisconsin woods of my childhood, the place where trees drop their leaves and obey the four seasons that many people insist are natural and essential. I am seventy miles from the Mexican line in this island of northern European obedience.

Yesterday, we left the highway at Catalina, Arizona, a small community burrowing into the rolling embrace of the Cañada. I have notebooks and pens, and Jack totes about a ton and a half of cameras and lenses. We went up the road to Charouleau Gap, a breech in Samaniego Ridge that permits the traveler to skip the long northern bend of the wash and drop directly into the heart of the canyon. As we walked, the sun burned through a blue sky, sweat rolled off our bodies, and our fifty-pound packs felt vicious on our shoulders.

The dry grass waved golden fingers, and a hawk drifted over the oak hillside. Four wooden stakes and brilliant yellow ribbons announced ground zero for some new demolition scheme on the land. We stopped and looked at survey markers like a physician fingering the hot spot on a lung X-ray.

Two does moved slowly up a small draw, alert at our presence but walking without panic. An ash burned yellow in the bottom of a small drainage.

After three miles, a four-wheel-drive truck came rumbling up the road. The man and woman were in their twenties and headed for Charouleau Gap to try a day hike on Samaniego Ridge. We climbed in back and rode up.

The red machine groaned up the pass and then parked. The man said he had bought the truck so he could look for gold. To date, he allowed, not much had come of his searching. A few small sums panning in waters like the Cañada—but he noted he had a friend who once found $120 in one day.

Have spent several days inspecting mines in the vicinity of Oracle.

Capitalists, they say, pursue a mine as one would an *IGNIS FAT- UUS*, the farther it is away and the more difficult to reach, the more fascinating it looks.

Arizona Weekly Star, April 28, 1881

We talk for a few minutes in the Gap. The Catalinas are many different mountains—cow country mountains, timber mountains, copper mountains, gold mountains, resort mountains.

And once in a great while, walking mountains.

We shoulder our packs and head in. The man and woman are the last people we will see for three days.

The Gap at first glance seems free of human beings and their ways. A century ago, the surrounding area was the playground for Pierre Charouleau, an illiterate Frenchman from Toulouse who had spent his early life roaming South and Central America. In 1873, his aunt, a Tucson pawnbroker, sent for him in Guatemala, gave him the ranch, and suddenly he was the lord of the key canyons backing the Catalinas. One fine June day in 1885, he and his friend John Spring, a Swiss who settled in southern Arizona, went into these mountains on a bear hunt. A Mexican herder followed the sign, and a dog, half wolfhound and half bulldog, strained at the leash.

They walk into the canyons and at 4,900 feet hit fresh tracks which lead upward into the mountain. After two miles, a sandy spot marks where the bear had rested. The canyon is dense with oak and juniper and brush. They tie the horses, let slip the dog who charges forward. In an instant, the animal returns with a broken paw and bloody ears. The bear crashes through the brush one hundred yards ahead and Spring fires, the bullet hitting with a thud, the bear giving off a shake but not slowing. The two men hear the animal moving up the hillside and rocks tumble down the ridge. At the top, he stops and looks down. Charouleau fires. The bear falls dead.

They are sleeping at the ranch that midnight when a vaquero enters and says a lion has taken a calf. At 3 a.m., they ride toward the kill. With dawn the lion returns, the guns roar, and for five minutes the big cat writhes in pain. A shot to the skull ends it.

Now Charouleau is nothing but a name. The Catalinas still have a few bears. Only the lion remains in strength, a beast who arcs across the public mind as a symbol of the mountain's wildness and across the ranchers' dreams as a crazed killer of stock.

A half mile down the road, we stop. Dead trees stroke the straw hillside with charred hands, the last memory of a fire. Jack sets up his tripod and hauls out the four-by-five camera. Something about the look of the scene, he says.

We are not much as hikers. Too many delays to look at dead trees or the patches of ground between my boots as I sit on a rock sipping morning coffee and wondering at the forms of fallen leaves.

We lack simple objectives, plotted routes, and easily stated desires. The Cañada del Oro, the Canyon of Gold, has felt the lash of other travelers. The tale first appeared in print in the *Arizona Weekly Star* of February 4, 1880.

About one hundred years ago the Jesuits held full sway over the population of this territory, and at that time they had large fields under cultivation and many men employed delving in the earth after the precious metals and turquoise stones. At that time the principle gold mines were situated in these mountains and there was a place called Nueva Mia Ciudad, having a monster church with a number of golden bells that were used to summon the laborers from the fields and mines, and a short distance from the city which was situated on a plateau, was a mountain that had a mine of such fabulous richness that the miners used to cut the gold out with a "hacheta." At the time of the Franciscans acquiring supremacy, the Jesuits fled, leaving the city destitute of population; before their flight they placed an iron door on the mine and secured it in such a manner that it would require a considerable time to unfasten it. There were only two entrances to the city and they also were closed and all traces obliterated so as to throw the Franciscans off the road to this Nueva Mia City.

The old article is reprinted in a yellow booklet published by a modern-day seeker of treasure. One day I was sitting with Buster Bailey, an old cowboy, under the ramada at his home in a junkyard when he hobbled into the house and fished the thing out. Buster maintains a private library of things he considers clues to the real West: old yellowed magazines with gunslingers on the cover, scribbled pages of cowboy songs, and odd items like the cluster of newspaper clippings on the Mine with the Iron Door. He allowed that he had some doubts about the legendary gold mine in the Cañada, but he did not seem anxious to argue away the possible bonanza. The booklet was real interesting, he said, and that was the way he wanted the mine to remain, a possibility sleeping somewhere up high on the mountain.

While we talked, a kid working at the junkyard came over and Buster showed him the book. The boy's eyes lit up and dreams of treasure suddenly fired in his face. He asked where he could get a copy. In that brief instant, a blind man would have sensed all the reasons why the mine lives on and on.

Now I sit in the Cañada del Oro and rifle the same pages, smiling at dreams of the main chance, the Big Rock Candy Mountain, the Days of '49, the Diamond As Big As The Ritz, the Glory Hole, the Bonanza, Paydirt, the Big Strike. In a nation propelled by money, this is the ultimate fuel source—gold, a metal all but useless except to jewelers and the dark wizards that float pounds, dollars, marks, and pesos.

For a century, Americans have searched the Cañada for the fabled Mine with the Iron Door, the secret vein of gold that supposedly stirred the blood of eighteenth-century Jesuits in southern Arizona.

With all this interest in fabled mines and wealthy priests, the early settlers had little time or inclination to note Indian use of the range—a use of which we know very little. In May 1894 some whites discovered a group of Papagos camped fourteen miles north of Tucson on the mountain. They were harvesting agaves (*Palmeri*). The hearts were cooked and dried in the spring as a food source for the desert people who lived to the west. Ropes were fashioned from the epidermis and fibers.

The Aravaipa band of the Western Apache came each year to the tip of Oracle Ridge and gathered acorns. In summer, they lived on top of the range and overlooked Tucson and the Santa Cruz Valley. The hunting was said to be good and they felt safe from their enemies: Mexicans, Americans, and Papagos.

In 1857, the Americans in Tucson sent word for the Apaches to meet with them in the Cañada del Oro. The tribesmen came to a place in the canyon they called "Urinating Toward the Water." The Americans gave them calico, pieces of copper wire (for bracelets), and some corn.

Potsherds are said to have been found under Bigelow Peak on the crest. Rock drawings and grinding holes exist a little above Molino Basin on the front side. And, of course, the bajada is pocked with prehistoric Hohokam village sites. That is about all we know of the thousands of years native people used the mountain.

Jack finishes his photos of dead trees reaching toward a sun they can no longer feel. We shoulder our packs and drop deep into the Cañada. We walk between two big ridges, Oracle on the east, Samaniego on the west. Before us looms the high country of the central range, a bubble of granite covered with fir, cedar, ponderosa, spruce, and snow.

The melt roars off boulders in the Cañada and we hop from rock to rock. The pack begins to feel like it belongs on the back.

And now for the story of the prospectors. . . . They told me they had come here on January 10, 1880, of the express purpose of exploring the mountains for the Nueva Mia Ciudad (Nine Mile City) and the mine with the iron door.

We had heard [they said] for many years of this place but did not put any credence on it; but about five months ago, we were traveling in Sonora on a prospecting tour, and one night we stopped near the town of Caborca with an old Mexican and his wife, and he was asking of Arizona and other matters and at last about mining. . . . He spoke up and asked us if we ever had heard of the mine with the iron door? We said yes but did not place any confidence in this story. He said, "I do because I have a book here which my grandfather had and he was one of the inhabitants of Nueva Mia city."

We became excited . . .

He went into the inner room and returned with a book covered with black cloth and leaves of parchment. . . . We judge it had at least 40 pages, and contained a kind of diary of events of those days, a history of his life, and a description of the Nueva Mia city and how to reach it; also full directions how to find the mine of the iron door. We offered to buy the book of the old man at a good round figure.

"No," he said, "I don't want to part with it for it is the last remnant of this old family but we could copy any part of it we wished."

We camped there for several days making extracts from the book, and one in particular which we now remember: "I worked today with ten other men and we took out 200 pounds of gold."

The forest of the canyon bottom swallows us. Sycamores stripped of leaves arch over our heads. The bark is splotched with dark gray, light gray, and cream yellow. The sky seems cement now and we stroll under a gray roof. There is not another soul in the big cut, and over the mountain crest a half million people go about their business and ignore what we now see.

They have been coming here for a long time. We move past fire rings left by deer hunters and campers but these penetrations are few and infrequent. The Cañada del Oro is the center of a century-long effort to bring the Catalinas to account. People have come here chasing the big money.

It is 1871 and Isaac Goldberg meets a former Apache captive in Tucson who tells him large chunks of gold are scattered about at the head of Cañada del Oro. Goldberg organizes a party of a dozen or so and follows the captive to the bonanza. The men find chunks of mica, and Goldberg decides he wants to return to Tucson.

Eight days later, the starving party stumbles out of the range. He scribbles an account: ". . . almost incredible hardships attended and encumbered our progress homeward—narrow steep trails between

Oracle Junction

dreadful abysses, exhausting tracts of rock sterility, and patches of brush so thick and thorny that our weary bodies lost their coverings, and our blistered feet their leather protectors. We were nearly naked, barefoot, and on the very brink of starvation, for we had no food except a small quantity of pinole and some wild grapes."

We see a different mountain.

Jack jokes about the mine and keeps a sharp eye for the Iron Door. I stagger onto some high ground of principle and argue that finding the fabled mine would be a disaster, a bit of information that would trigger a nuclear-sized strike of greed, big shovels, tailings, roads, bulldozers, and people.

He dismisses these trivial points and explains that we will keep the lode a secret and steal into the canyon every couple of months for a few chunks of gold to toss to our creditors.

The plan is elaborate as he spins it out on the trail in the Cañada. My role in this new enterprise, he brightens, entails being the pachyderm, an obedient dumb beast that will trudge the narrow, steep trails across exhausting tracts of sterility and hop along the edge of the dreadful abysses. It is my destiny, he smiles, some fate cooked up for me in a previous life, and one that may spare me a future return as a caterpillar, beetle, or public official.

On a winter day under a soggy gray sky, the whole scam doesn't sound half bad. But no one ever seems to take a few chunks of anything and leave the rest.

I remember once wintering on a New England farm where the heat came from firewood and the wood came from the axe and the saw and long hours in the forest. The January days snapped with air brittle at thirty below zero, and I learned one simple thing: not to waste firewood.

Across the road from the 150-year-old farm, two local guys worked like slaves on a small portable sawmill. They whacked trees off with gusto and snaked logs out of the woods. When they got through, the scene looked like hell. They weren't trying to feed a pot-bellied stove. They were busy converting maples to boards and then small staves for the wooden platforms found on loading docks. They were driven by creditors, visions of items they had seen in stores or on television, and they cut every damn tree they could wrestle off the tract.

The gold mine of the Cañada is a thing with no checks built in to temper the pursuit. The fabled hole in the mountain means wealth, not a rack of logs slowly burning in a pot-bellied stove as frost cakes on the windows. Not many have come to this range simply to slake a thirst or fill an empty belly or chase the chill from a room. They have come here with larger dreams. As they toil on the mountain chasing gold or cattle or sizing up trees for lumber, they tend to fall in love with the place. But love is not enough to protect a mountain.

The hunger for the big strike roars in the old accounts. The *Arizona Weekly Star* on July 28, 1881, ticked off the mining hopes for Oracle Ridge. One hole boasted a "force of 40 men" and the prime mover in such assaults was not the local boys, but "Eastern parties" or "San Francisco capitalists." They did not simply dig; rather, "the work will be prosecuted unremittingly." And no one wasted any time fretting about maiming the land because the writer asserted there was a "never failing stream of water, and grass and timber all around." The piece ended with a hymn to the possibilities of the range:

There are few mining districts which present as many attractive features as the Santa Catalinas, or as great a diversity of minerals. Wood, water, and the prime necessities for profitable mining, are abundant and easily obtained, and the would be investor, within a radius of a few miles can have his choice of gold, silver or copper properties.

Resort development beneath Pusch Ridge

There is something about the possibilities of the Cañada and adjacent ridges that fired up our ancestors to a frenzy worthy of a rat in heat. A visitor in August 1881 practically wept over the slow pace of hacking the mountain into money:

Through this whole mineral district [Oracle Ridge], strewn with promising mines as it is, not more than ten properties are being now developed and not a single mill is doing anything to add to the bullion product of the world. If this belt were in California, the cheerful clatter of the stamps would awaken the echoes on every hillside and canyon, and all would be bustle and clatter where now is solitude . . .

    The black bear, wildcat and coyote are occasionally encountered; but such varmints are being rapidly thinned out.

The miners of the late nineteenth century did not fail to provide a clatter in the mountains from lack of trying. Thousands of cords of big oak vanished from the north side to fuel a smelter in Mammoth. Miners became artists at filing mineral claims so that they could cut off the timber. The first sawmill in Alder Canyon two miles below what is now Summerhaven fired up in the early 1880s and an 1882 account pegged production at 5,000 board feet per day. In 1916, the three-ton boiler was dragged up to Summerhaven itself—a feat that took three months.

The mountain saved itself from these hungry saws and axes. The steep slopes finally convinced local entrepreneurs that lumber could be more cheaply imported from the West Coast than timbered off the Catalinas.

But the dream of wealth kept bewitching people. In 1916 an old man spent his last winter on earth at Campo Bonito just below Oracle Ridge. When he was born in 1846 in LeClaire, Iowa, they called him William Frederick Cody, and when he died in 1917 he was known all over the world as Buffalo Bill. He made his mark as a pony express rider, scout, Indian fighter, buffalo hunter, and finally as the hero of dozens of dime novels and as a showman inventing the web of fantasy we now devour in bad books and cheer at rodeos. He sensed the theater of the West, and he consciously carved out good roles for himself.

In 1876, a few weeks after Custer's command died at the Little Bighorn, Cody shot and killed a Cheyenne subchief, Yellow Hair. This became known in the press of the day as the first scalp for Custer. Cody left a stage show in the East to join the campaign and wore one of his stage costumes for the combat—a black velvet Mexican vaquero outfit with a scarlet sash and trimmed in silver buttons and lace.

He never faltered in his sense of the West as theater. Once in "The Wild West," he employed Sitting Bull as a spectacle in his road productions (whatever Cody was doing the word "show" was never used in any of the publicity). When Sitting Bull was murdered in 1890 by Indian police, his horse from the "Wild West" tour, a gift from Buffalo Bill, apparently sensed some cue from the old act in the shooting and sat down in the middle of the flying bullets and raised one hoof. The Indian police were terrified, thinking Sitting Bull's spirit had entered the horse. Cody later retrieved the beast and used him in the tour.

He guided European princes on Western hunts, hobnobbed with rich and titled people on two continents, and had a genius for losing money in mining ventures. He was the perfect hero for the late nineteenth century, part Kit Carson, part P.T. Barnum.

By 1916, he was wintering on Oracle Ridge, hoping he'd find the heart of gold that would repair his finances and restore his grip on his private world. He had this notion of having a rich mine in the sunny Southwest and a big ranch in the cool Northwest. He had first come to Oracle in 1911 and was cheered by all thirty-five inhabitants of the place. If there was a symbol of what people wanted the West to be—freedom, daring, the hunt, and the long ride—Cody was it.

Initially, he became interested in the prospects of the Catalinas when William Neal, an old scout, bewitched him with the notion of discovering the Mine with the Iron Door. Neal was convinced that a great earthquake in 1887 had buried the mine. From that first speculation, Cody went on to spend thousands searching for gold in the Catalinas. He seemed to like the area—in 1912 at Christmas he played Santa Claus for 200 children rounded up from the camps and ranches for fifty miles around. He squandered $500,000 in local mining ventures.

The allure of the big strike was too powerful for Cody to ever let go. In 1914, he is busy touring with his "Wild West" as part of the Sells-Floto Circus and his letters to his partners back in Oracle are scribbled on hotel stationery from San Francisco, Denver, and Washington. He is making motion pictures to get together another bankroll.

He advises his men at Campo Bonito to "hang on and just wait a few weeks until I can get my pictures on the road and then I will show our Sells-Floto 'Buffalo Bill Show' in Albuquerque . . . El Paso . . . Douglas . . . Tucson. I haven't got any money out of the moving pictures yet, but I believe I will pretty soon."

By the last winter of his life in 1916, the buffalo was practically extinct, the Indians tame, Sitting Bull murdered, and the hunting grounds of his youth caged behind barbed wire. Time was running out for Cody's sense of the West as a place he could always count on to repair his life and fortune. While he was at Campo Bonito that winter a Mexican trapped a big jaguar in upper Cañada del Oro. He skinned the beast and then traveled over the ridge and presented the trophy to Buffalo Bill, a living relic of something already known as the Old West.

The mine, a hope of tungsten, silver, and gold, did not pan out. That Christmas Cody once again dressed as Santa Claus for the local children. The story goes that he became very tired and hot in his costume and went outside and sat on a rock. He caught pneumonia. A month later he died and was buried on Lookout Mountain in Colorado.

Some people in Oracle made a kind of museum of the gear he left behind. His life ended as it had begun, a hunger for the freedom of the West that seemed constantly to betray itself as the hunt led to extinction of the game, the wars led to the end of the independent life of the tribesmen, and the mines led to either personal ruin when the holes proved barren or the ruin of mountains when the flecks of precious metals happened to be discovered.

In the Cañada del Oro, the basic drives of my nation and myself have been acted out for over a century in a search for an escape from our lives and an entrance into the place of appetites with no limit.

In some ways, I am too far gone to sympathize with the hungers of my own culture even though these impulses rumble through my life as well. Seven days ago, I quit my job and walked out into a small pile of savings and no work. This kind of foolishness strikes me every two or three years, and I have learned there is no help for it but leaving and walking into the wild ground. And now I stumble up the canyon looking for birds and eating silence and averting my eyes from any mines with iron doors.

When we arrived in the Cañada del Oro, from the description we found it would be necessary to proceed on foot from this point, and, turning our horses and burros loose to shift for themselves, we shouldered our picks and took the middle canyon that led in an easterly direction from Cañada del Oro. It was about noon as we started up the canyon, and we were not quite sure that we would reach the place where water was said to exist the year round by our description, but we plodded onward and upward over the largest boulders, now passing through places where the very top of the canyon would fairly join, and then opening out larger in box shape. Toward evening we came to a living spring of water and here we camped for the night.

Everything passed off finely that night with the exception of bears coming uncomfortably close, and the thrilling cry of the panther.

The Cañada runs high as we slowly walk from its oak mouth to its pine top. Once the settlers searching for the idea of a ranch or the hope of a big strike homesteaded the small grassy openings of the forest. Two sections of stovepipe rust by the trail.

A visitor to the ridge in the 1880s sized up the locals as a credit to the human race and certainly good enough for Arizona.

The frontier life of the Pacific Coast used in pioneer days to be cursed by the prevalence of an uncouth class known under the generic name of "pikes." I have seen none of that hoggish species on the frontier of Arizona. On this trip, in particular, I met no man, no matter how rude his exterior might be, who was not as to manners and courtesies extended to strangers one of nature's noblemen; and as such—when mated to such women as I have had the good fortune to meet in the Santa Catalinas—will the splendid superstructure of our great Southwestern mineral empire be built up.

The light showers down with a green cast that means a storm and every slip of life glows under its faint rays. We fall into a moving daze where nothing is happening, and we are silenced by the rush of sights and lack of events.

Quick forms nag at the corner of the eye and we wheel to glimpse six coatis (*Nasua nasua*) racing through the brush. The dark brown coats shine against the dead carpet of leaves.

Coati bands range up to fifty members and the animals are creatures of Mexico's Sierra Madre with the Catalinas close to their northern frontier (although they've been sighted a hundred miles to the north). The animals run about forty-one inches long and weigh in at around twenty-five pounds. They are the creatures no one is prepared for, animals described as raccoonlike but when sighted they look like something else again. The movement is the thing, that tail held high, the strange lope that gives them the look of furry serpents rolling and writhing across the oak woodland.

You walk out into your American woods and suddenly the branches part and there stands a unicorn. That is the feel of sighting a coati.

When I was fifteen on a deer hunt, I saw my first band of coatis grazing a grassy slope across a draw. I was tired, armed with a .303 British Enfield from the last good war and a peanut butter sandwich. I was instantly filled with a desire to see them more closely. I lifted my rifle and fired and one fell dead.

The band scattered into the brush and I worked across the gulch and stood over the small brown body. The bag of fur bleeding on the hill of golden grass was not much to see. I had shot away the thing that interested me.

After the small family of six flee our presence, Jack and I start to babble. We have gone long years without stumbling on such a band, and that somehow makes the beasts important. But there is something else going on, something that keeps us talking for minute after minute as we move up the trail, something we cannot quite put our fingers on.

It is 2:30 in the afternoon on a December day as a storm builds over the Cañada del Oro and we have just watched six coatis run in panic from our presence. If I said that the Santa Catalina Mountains should be preserved inviolate so that such moments would always be possible, not many people would think much of the argument. But that is exactly what I think.

I am perfectly willing to accept the proposition that coatis have no role in any useful work known on the surface of the earth, that they are the small mammal equivalent of urban planners, sociopaths, newspaper owners, and federal bureaucrats.

I just sense I need them. They tell me I will never know the world they know. And this fact reassures me that there is more to life than I will ever imagine.

We pitch camp high in the Cañada at a point under the Reef of Rocks where the oak begins to surrender ground to the coniferous forest of the upper mountain. Our tent is barely a shelter, a floorless canopy of nylon pegged in four corners, held up by a single pole and gaping a foot off the ground around the bottom. The sky finally delivers the storm, and we lay in our bags listening to the wind whip the trees and the rain pelt the fabric over our heads.

After midnight, the storm regroups and water beats against the tent. I lay there staring into the darkness and listening to the roar of the Cañada and the drip, drip, drip of beads of water falling off the edge of the nylon six inches from my head.

I flash my light and catch a scene of dark oaks with weathered bark glistening like oiled muscle in the downpour.

In the morning we cooked our breakfast and as we sat down to partake of it we took our directions and examined them. . . . We followed up this large canyon about four miles, when we came to where it divided into two. We took the right hand one and in the course of half an hour or so we came to where the canyon suddenly became walled in on the three sides and, after considerable hunting, we discovered what seemed to be an old stairway cut in the rocks; we had a terrible time in getting up them as they were partly obliterated . . . but we reached a shelving rock and on the face of the perpendicular wall was an opening that would admit of an entrance of a full grown person. . . . We took some candles from our pack;

unslung our "Henrys" in case of emergency and passed in the opening. We had not gotten far when a flock of bats commenced circling around us, attracted by our lights. . . . And in one place we noticed an inscription engraved in the wall in Latin—*Dominus vobiscum*, and from that we began to get more confidence we were on the right track. In about an hour we saw light ahead, and down about 200 feet below us was the finest scenery that we ever beheld. It was a tract of land covered with pine and oaks, broken by small hills, and through it passed a stream of water that glistened like silver. . . . We sat down at the bottom for some time examining our directions: they told us that by traveling in an easterly direction we would come to the Nueva Mia Ciudad. They did not give us the distance so we concluded that we would find water and pitch our stakes for the night. In about 20 minutes, we came to the stream of water that was mentioned before; it was literally alive with trout . . . as we were cleaning them we noticed shining particles in the stream. We took our bread pan and washed it and in it was about a dollar's worth of gold.

The rain lets up at dawn and we breakfast under cold, gray skies. To the east, Oracle Ridge floats in and out of cloud cover. Ahead, the high point of the range, Mt. Lemmon, hides in a layer of white. The ridge provided the first gateway to the high country and hosted the typical lacerations favored by nineteenth-century mountaineers—mines.

In March 1881, John Gill Lemmon and his bride, Sarah Plummer Lemmon, got off the train in Tucson. Pioneer botanists from California, they looked up at the 9,000-foot Catalinas and wanted to go there and name the plants. For weeks they puzzled out the canyons of the front range on the mountains' south side and could find no easy route to the high country. People in town told them to look up Emerson Oliver Stratton, a rancher and mine owner living on the slopes of the mountain's north side.

Lemmon arrived at Stratton's ranch riding a horse. His wife walked behind him. Stratton was the western pioneer, a man on the move, an optimist who did not so much put down roots as send out feelers for business deals, ventures, and dreams of the big strike. He tried bookkeeping in California, moved to Lima, Peru, and opened a roller rink, spent some time helping build a railroad in the Andes, manned a stage stop at Maricopa Wells west of Phoenix, served as undersheriff of Pinal County, grubstaked prospectors that combed the back country, opened up a homestead and went bust, plunged repeatedly into mining ventures and went bust, bagged political appointments such as county assessor, and just generally kept an eye peeled for the Big Rock Candy Mountain. By the time the Lemmons dropped in, Stratton had gotten the drift of his life: he called his ranch Pandora.

Lemmon himself was not a thrill-seeking mountaineer. A survivor of Andersonville prison in the Civil War, he came home a wreck. After a year of recovery, he still weighed ninety pounds.

"I first groped about the yard," he wrote later, "upheld by the fence rail. The next day I was able to walk a little way alone, being greatly stimulated by unrecognizable plants. In a few days, I could go further, assisted by my aged mother."

This past left Lemmon a bit on the odd side—"nervous and excitable in a very unfortunate way . . . ," as one acquaintance put it. Hunting for plants new to science put Lemmon back on the edges of the real world. By the time he showed up at Stratton's ranch just below Oracle Ridge, he was forty-nine years old, his new wife forty-six.

They rode horses up the ridge to the top, a journey that provided a tour through Arizona's favorite form of nineteenth-century larceny, mining.

Just over the slopes from where Jack and I walk in the Cañada del Oro sleeps the Apache Girl, an 1880s gouge in the mountain. John P. Zimmerman and Sam Parkinson loved the mine because they figured the hole would put them on easy street. When the vein of gold quickly petered out, they saw their diggings in a new light. They were part of a wave of prospectors that slammed against the mountain in the 1880s and 1890s, men who believed any pile of rocks that big had to hold a bonanza.

One day a man came out from Tucson and expressed an interest in the Apache Girl. Zimmerman and Parkinson showed him their dump, a heap liberally salted with gold specimens. Then they led him crashing through the dense oak thickets to a second dump and a third.

Naturally, the three dumps were all the same one. The man from Tucson was too busy huffing and puffing up the mountainside to notice. He bought himself a gold mine. Zimmerman and Parkinson hit the road.

Lemmon and his party did a little better. Most of the way up Oracle Ridge, they rode into Dan Saddle and the two botanists came alive. Lemmon grabbed a branch and shouted, "All hats off!" His hand held the needles of a new species for his list, *Pinus Arizonica*, a tree "for which I had so long been in search."

Eventually, the group got to the summit, a 9,157-foot peak. Stratton and the Lemmons carved their names on a big tree and Stratton named the spot Mt. Lemmon after Mrs. Lemmon. The tree is gone, but the name has stuck.

The two botanists found more than one hundred plants new to science in the Catalinas and neighboring ranges. Stratton finally had his luck turn and peddled a mine site that still bears his name on Oracle Ridge. He split for the West Coast and built a nice house in San Francisco.

As we hike up the Cañada, I savor these old tales of exploration and greed. A hundred years ago, wilderness meant a condition that must be erased and mountains meant obstacles and nuisances that might be forgiven for existing if they coughed up a fortune in gold. I walk on the far side of a great divide, a chasm that opened up in the twentieth century when people noticed that their ideas and ways of using land would lead to a country with no real land left at all. Lemmon and Stratton enjoyed a different country where such thoughts hardly occurred and were readily dismissed.

In the cliffs up ahead, that band of prospectors claimed to the *Arizona Weekly Star* in 1880 that they had discovered the Mine with the Iron Door that would deliver wealth beyond dreams. Now I look at the same terrain and see the same rusted door as a gaping hole leading to bad times. To our left Marble Peak towers, a rise huddled on a sizeable copper deposit [2.28%] that will someday explode into a frenzy of activity when that mystery beast, the global market, gets a deep itch to gorge on more of the metal. So Stratton's world is not yet dead, and my scheme for things remains a bit of whimsy easily bulldozed out of the way by the rush of twentieth-century energy.

Before daybreak we had our breakfasts and had everything packed for an early start. We set our compass and started easterly, and had not gone more than a mile before we came onto the ruins, which, as we proceeded grew larger and could be seen for two miles in width. . . . We came upon a stone building (granite and marble) that was in a fair state of preservation . . . ; the structure was something after the style of the old Cocospari church in Sonora, and we decided that this must have been the place of worship of the people of this once populous city . . .

We then changed our camping ground and commenced looking for the mine with the iron door and after three days found it. The old door was eaten off by rust. . . . We were afraid to enter for fear of wild beasts; but the love of excitement got the best of us and we entered. We saw at the commencement that the vein was about ten inches wide. . . . We found some old iron resembling in shape the pick, we took it up and struck it into the vein and to our amazement gold rolled down in nuggets to the floor. [Here the two men unpacked from their burros and showed me, I should judge, 100 pounds of pure gold in nuggets.]

I and my partner leave tomorrow for Nine Mile City. If a lie, we will stand it; if not, so much the better. I tell you those gold nuggets gave us a good deal of faith; and further, I am one of the oldest prospectors in these mountains, and I have never known anyone to go up these canyons.

I will write as soon as I return.

The fable of the Mine with the Iron Door may outlast the mountains. When the Jesuits entered this area, they introduced irrigated agriculture with European crops like wheat. Using Indian labor they built big churches out of mud. The Americans who came a century later refused to believe so simple an explanation for the large ruins. Listen to the prospectus of the Arizona Advancement Company in 1897:

We do not doubt they availed themselves freely of nature's treasures and that the noble edifices, whose ruins we behold today with admiration and wonder, were built in great part from clandestine mining operations.

In 1923, Harold Bell Wright pens a novel entitled *The Mine with the Iron Door*. A book in 1933 says an old Opata Indian named Calisatro who lives in Tumacacori knows of the mine. Maps float around giving the location. In the 1950s, a Spanish forge is said to be found in the canyon.

Down below, in the valley, these dreams of the quick buck still thrive. Up here they are small moments of nonsense easily overwhelmed by the thickening forest in the upper canyon, by the sputter of water leaping off the boulders.

To the west of the Santa Catalinas flows the Santa Cruz River, the major channel draining the big valley where Tucson now sprawls. On a clear day from the high country, the eye travels fifty to one hundred miles, dancing over the desert floor that laps against range after range of mountains. I see beauty.

Others see something else:

LOST MINES OF THE SANTA CRUZ VALLEY

The Mine With The Iron Door

Escalante Mine

Treasure of Del Rio

La Esmeralda Mine

Lost Arivaca Mine

Lost Vampire Mine

The Virgin of Guadalupe Mine

La Purisima Concepcion Mine

Lost Treasure of Tumacacori

The San Pedro Mine

Lost Bell of Tumacacori

Opata Silver Mine

Treasure of the Padres

Lost Bells of Guevavi

Guevavi Treasure

The day grows colder and the rain begins again and drifts toward snow. We leave the shoulder of the stream and cut up the hillside following a fork to Shovel Springs. Our breath comes harder; the storm slaps our faces.

Above the trickle of the spring sits a small, pale green cabin. We enter, dump our packs, and break out the stove.

The forest outside the small cabin looks big and immortal but in 1921, in this reach 10,000 acres of the Cañada burned for almost a week. Those were the early days of fire fighting and the Army Air Corps, eager to find work once World War I ended, loaned men and machines to the Forest Service as fire spotters. The squads (commanded at the time by Col. Hap Arnold) darted in and out of narrow mountain canyons training for a face-off with the next Red Baron. Without radios, the craft had to fly over fire spotters in the ground towers when they sighted a blaze and drop the written message in tin cans or try their luck with tiny parachutes. By 1921, the Army was frolicking in the skies of the Catalinas.

We climb out of the Cañada around noon and walk the ridge toward Lemmon. The ground becomes snow and the air a kind of fog. We round a bend and meet big trees blackened by some lightning strike. The wind rushes up the mountain, wisping clouds through the dead grip of the slaughtered forest.

The boots leave intricate tread marks in the snow. Big Douglas firs stand like lords and there is no sound but the crunch of our steps. We follow the Trico Electric line, a wide scar bringing power up the mountain. We see no tracks and the birds have fallen silent.

The storm rolls in and out, each pulse a little stronger. We hit the Lemmon trail, a strand winding through the trees down to Romero Pass at 6,000 feet.

Our spirits brighten at the ease of the downhill and we alter plans every few minutes as vistas flash through partings of the clouds.

At a series of palisades over Romero Canyon we throw our bags down, pitch the tent, and settle in for the blow.

The afternoon churns wisps of cloud out of the folds of the canyons as the mountain breathes the weather back toward the sky. Cathedral, Kimball, and Table all poke in and out of view. The clouds suddenly become ropes hugging the slopes and then in an instant they rise, reach some critical mass, and everything goes blank as a brief whiteout whips through our camp.

Night falls and we huddle in our bags devouring freeze-dried dinners. Then the rain begins and goes to ice. We talk and then abandon that and let the storm fill our minds.

The mountain and the storm imprison me in my sleeping bag and I ransack memory as a way to march across the long dark hours. I am bored, but the emptiness takes hold like a drug. The cold wind whips me back to the Wisconsin of my childhood.

She was old when I first met her, a small, smiling woman in her seventies with a lifetime behind her of squeezing a living from a Jackson County farm. Rose could do a lot of things but mainly she could fish, and when people mentioned her name they quickly followed with talk of her skill with a cane pole.

The air quakes with mosquitoes, and frogs croak in the murk of the cranberry bog. Rose baits a hook, tosses out the line and whomp! A bullhead bolts down the bait. She flings the small mud-colored fish on the bank, carefully grabs the body behind the sharp spines, and with a fluid movement slips the fish off the hook and pitches it into a waiting barrel.

Her face is lines, her hands hard with calluses, and her smile serene. Sometimes on a summer evening, she will pull in 500 bull-heads from the bog, a hell of a lot of skinning and cleaning. No matter.

Or it is midday by a small pond abutting a meadow. Dead trees dot the glass surface of the water. Rose tosses out a line and instantly a sunfish or bluegill takes the bait.

She is a genius at communicating with crappies, bluegills, suck-ers, bullheads, small bass—all the endless brands of pan fish that thrive in warm, muddy water. The day slips along and there is no sound louder than a breeze working through the oaks, the slap of bait hitting the water. She does not speak much.

I am ten years old and realize I am witnessing some kind of brilliance. Rose does not simply belong here. She is at one with the landscape she works, and after a while she seems to disappear from view, a woman who joins with the pond and meadow and woods.

It is morning and we are on the banks of the Black River and the sky leans down close to the land, heavy with dark clouds. The heat goes out of the air and Rose cracks dry branches over her knee and hunkers to make a fire. I watch closely as she pulls a small scrap of metal from her pocket. There is a rasp of sound, a spark, and then a flame. I have just seen my first human being beckon fire forth with a flint.

The tent shifts and sways with the wind. We are camped in the lee of a rock on the cliffs over Romero but the storm hunts us even here.

I look at my watch: 2:30 a.m. I have to urinate and the roar outside gives me little hope. The rain has gone to ice and then departed and a three-quarter moon beams down on the mountain painting the ground milk.

I pull on my boots and enter the night wearing shorts and a shirt. Instantly, I begin to shudder as the cold digs deep into my muscle. The entire range stretches to the west, a rock spine of peaks bathing in light. The city glows with electric fire but makes no sound. I shake in the cold and seek the warmer days.

Summer slips away and I follow the old man through the brush understory of the forest. He speaks with a German ring to his English and calls himself Gust. He is gaining on eighty years and has spent his life on a small Jackson County farm that backs on miles of forest.

He has never married. One day each week he bakes seven loaves of bread. Each fall he pockets four or five cartridges and goes into the timber after his deer. Blackberries and raspberries he gathers from the brambles by the bucketfull, and once every week or two he drives slowly into Black River Falls and strides into a saloon. He always orders a peppermint schnapps.

He loves to tell stories and the stories are tall. He is deer hunting and climbs up into an oak to wait out the game. Sleep takes him and he falls into a dream. When he awakens, his gun is warm and a dead buck lies sprawled before him. Red stains reach like ribbons on the snow.

Sometimes he does not talk at all.

We walk with few words as if speech were a felony. A red fox bolts from the cover and is gone. Gust stoops and plucks a wild strawberry and offers it to me. I hesitate over eating something that has not come from a grocery store. I wonder if it is clean.

Blueberries suddenly carpet the ground. We bend low and slowly fill our buckets. Gust dreams of pies.

In the winter, I am trapped in the Chicago apartment. A package arrives. I rip it open and find Gust has sent a box of butternuts. They are large, the hulls covered with a soft brown hair. I take the box down into the basement and bust one open with a hammer.

I stand and eat the rich nut under the dangling light bulb while the furnace roars against the cold of a January day. For months I will see nothing but straight streets, hear little but the rumble of traffic and the roar of the subway. I hoard the sack of nuts.

I am almost thirty years older now and I linger outside the tent on the mountain, shaking from the cold and stunned by the beauty. I lie in a tent for ten or twelve hours and listen to the storm and wander through Wisconsin.

The thing began very early when I was not paying attention. A page in a book, an old woman tossing a line over the still green water, the fox running red through the bramble.

I have read the conservation tracts, plundered the ecology books, paid dues to societies that talk to congressional committees and save wild ground and wild animals. My mailbox is stuffed with letters begging for whales, seal pups, California condors, grizzly bears, Nebraska rivers, southern swamps, western mountains, black-footed ferrets, and lonely groves of redwoods.

Mule deer, Sabino Canyon

All these matters seem worthy but somehow make me feel like I have just gone to church.

I am forty years old, the ground is hard, the air brittle with the cold, and the mountain is rubbing against the wind in the night. Wisconsin is 2,000 miles away from my feet and seconds away from my mind.

There are words I mouth: conservation, ecology, wilderness areas, national parks, endangered species, diversity, ecosystem, biome, biosphere. I approve. Yes, yes. I'll sign your petition, write the congressman maybe, join the organization.

But these matters are a kind of polite conversation in a clean, well-appointed room. The chairs are comfortable but the air lacks scent and things feel dull to the touch. These things do not move me and do not bring me to the mountain.

With dawn clouds boil over Cathedral Peak, and the city begins to rumble with its work. The tent stands as a blue cone of ice. To the northwest, clouds lay like paste over the Tortolitas. The Cañada del Oro runs slick with water. On the bajadas I can see dirt roads raking across the desert and the roads are lined with blueprints for new houses and factories.

We pack up around noon, drop down to Romero Pass, and exit out the West Branch of Sabino. We cut across the basin at dusk and see eight deer feeding on the hills of gold.

Gold has been found in the Catalinas, just 30 miles north of Tucson, according to information given out last night. The ore in pockets is said to be so rich that vision of the forty-niners, Virginia City and the Comstock came before the sober eyes of Tucsonans discussing the question and speculating as to whether this city will be the Mecca for a gold stampede. . . .

When seen last night, exhibited samples of the ore . . . had tested 256 ounces of silver and 1200 ounces of gold, or approximately $26,000 to the ton.

Prospector, July 31, 1922

BUSTER'S MOUNTAIN

One who views the Santa Catalina range from the side facing Tucson—rugged, verdureless, and precipitous as it appears—would scarcely suspect that just beyond its forbidding though picturesque crest stretches in verdant beauty a slope of country that has in its natural state many of the features of a terrestrial paradise; where the summer's sun imparts only a genial warmth; where flowery mesas, "green and of mild declivity," fanned by refreshing breezes, watered by living springs and babbling brooks, and shaded by noble oaks, spread their vast though unsurveyed acres through a wide extent of pastoral country, as yet but slightly utilized by man.

Having heard of this favored locality, so near our verdureless village, I thought a brief surcease from business cares could be better spent there than in the long and expensive trip to California.

Buster Bailey

The blue eyes are going now, the knee's shot, the years are catching up. The hands are strong with thick fingers and wrists, the skin scarred with a lifetime of barbed wire, broken transmissions, and wells that needed fixing.

Dogs mill under the table in the shack and black coffee steams from mugs bought fifty years ago at Ronstadt's Hardware. The face grins and the old man throws out a song:

Jack of Diamonds, Jack of Diamonds,
I've known you of old.
You've robbed my poor pockets of silver and gold.
It's the whiskey, you villain, you've been my downfall,
You have kicked me and cuffed me but I love you for all.

I sit there and wonder why I have knocked at this door. My idea of a good time is hiking a trail with a heavy pack or thrashing through the brush watching birds watch me. The old man roams his seventies now and thinks birds are something you eat and backpackers are something you run out of the country. I have come to his place because of the mountain, because people have said to me there is this man you must talk to, this old man who knows that mountain. I sip the strong coffee and the old man and I study each other's moves.

The voice floats over the one-room home full of Old Fitzgerald bottles, four mutts (all females) used to this music, over the bed that came from the dump and the blankets that came from the dump, over the stove from the dump, the refrigerator from the dump, over a world hauled up from the dump in trip after trip in an old Chevy pickup bought from a wrecker in 1960.

Out the door, the freeway roars with traffic and past the cement road, houses spread mile after mile until they slap up against the western snout of the Santa Catalina Mountains. He has done things to that mountain I don't like—run cows that crop the range down toward ruin, butchered mesquite like so many weeds in his way. He curses the Forest Service and every sane gesture toward managing the public ground so that the land might persist and heal.

And I am his nightmare vision of the future, the guy from the city that considers the range a kind of toy where one can go and play wilderness. I am the person who insists on the rules, the restrictions, the dreaded choke hold on an old way of life that has been his life.

The old man keeps singing, his eyes softly focused, his head cocked as he pitches his message at a century that rips by on the freeway at sixty miles per hour.

It'll make you sick and it'll make you so poor,
It'll make you go uuuuuuaghhhhhhhh!! all over the floor.
There goes the old jailer that I damned near forgot,
He's the dirtiest old bastard of the whole lot.
He'll rifle your pockets, your clothes he will sell,
And get drunk on the money, goddamn him to hell.

The words drift away and the dogs snap and snarl underfoot as they jockey for his attention. He loves dogs, has a whole book pasted with clippings from the newspapers and magazines, old yellowed scraps of things going back decades where a dog saves someone's life, or befriends someone, or gets left behind and makes a cross-country journey pursuing his owners to their new town or state. He is real big on that kind of tale.

The mountain stands like a faint wall struggling through the city's smog and dust and fumes. The old man likes the mountain, too.

"I didn't build that damn mountain," he offers, "but I lived on it a few days. I know one thing. They've fucked it up."

But then, he's seen them mess up a lot of things. When he came into this country in June of 1927, a sixteen-year-old kid, fresh from around Van Horn, Texas, the place had a different look to it. Now his time has gone, and he lives in a present he does not like.

He has become a footnote. Up on the mountain, there is a Buster Spring and above Buster Spring rolls Buster Mountain. For the old man this seems a trifle strange. He is Buster Bailey, seventy some years old, a man living in a junkyard with a household bagged at the dump. In a city of half a million, he is a ghost. And now they've gone and made him into some kind of landmark.

A new bridge over Cañada del Oro on the Oracle Highway swallowed the land he settled as a boy in 1927. The new Catalina State Park spreading against the north side of the range has entombed the ranches he worked and built in the thirties. Mesquite roots chew the soil of his old corrals, hackberry spreads over the spot where he once put his still, and a bulldozer has sliced off his old house lest it blemish the natural setting.

"Every time they close out a productive ranch for homes," he suddenly flares, "they're only fucking themselves."

He hates the homes, he hates the factories, he hates the fancy stores, he hates the Forest Service and the backpackers and the wilderness designations that lock up his old stomping ground.

He hates everything that has come between him and that mountain. I listen in silence to the old man's theater of anger.

"One of the things that pisses me off," he snorts, "is the politicians and their beautiful mountain lions. I hope one of those bastards scratch their balls off."

Christ, he remembers one spring in 1932 or 1933 when lions took twenty-two colts up there. He remembers a lot of things.

"Used to be," he sighs, thinking of the Tucson of his youth, "you walked up on A Mountain and you looked down on the Santa Cruz River and it was the prettiest son of a bitch you ever saw. Green with trees. You went up the Rillito and it was gardens and cattle until it hit the rocks at Tanque Verde Falls."

Jesus, the thought pains him worse than 80 proof whiskey, and as a former bootlegger, he is hell on weak whiskey.

"You don't drink 80 proof," he explains patiently as if trying to educate a child, "if you want to stay well."

The dogs hop on the bed and settle in. The old man gets up and shuffles across the room with his game leg. He is still big, the gut slops over the belt, the shoulders are square, and the head is erect. He grabs a fistfull of harps and pitches them on the table. They land with a thud between the mugs of murderous coffee and a half-empty bottle of Old Fitzgerald. He tilts back his head and says:

If any you fellows get to heaven just do this one thing pards,
Look up that fellow who invented that coffee
and give him my regards.

Smiling at the thought, he punches the harp into his mouth and suddenly a train roars out. First, the engine wheezes as it builds up steam, then the big wheels start slowly rolling, the pace picks up, and the thing screams down the tracks. The sound has a melody but seems to hang in the air of the shack like a stalled idea. Then his foot starts tapping, the dogs rise and stir, the foot thumps and thumps, and the train pouring from his mouth picks up steam, moves, and storms out the door.

Buster Bailey is intent upon his journey. The thick fingers bury the tiny harp, the eyes squint, and the gray hair tumbles down his forehead.

"I never did get to be one of the best," he allows. "I've been in remote places where you didn't see a soul for thirty days, so you had to do something to amuse yourself."

He is conscious of his position in a kind of long decline. When he entered this country, he found the real old-time cowboys, the

Road work near Bailey's ranch

men who had arrived with settlement, and he is quick to declare that he is not of their mettle. But he is keen on the distinction between his life's work and the current age of drugstore cowboys and city people walking around in funny hats and Levis.

I fumble around trying to discover what the big rock pile means to the cantankerous old man. He looks at me like I'm a certifiable idiot.

"That old mountain," he almost whispers, "*that's been the beauty thing of my life.*"

Now he has about run out his string. "When you get to where you can't ride," he barks, "and can't do anything you used to do, . . . well, life ain't very interesting anymore." But he keeps hanging in there. He's got these prejudices to keep the juices flowing. Take cactus.

"I hate the fucking cactus," he beams. "When I ran the ranch I went around with an ax and a shovel. Prickly pear, they're just taking over the country. Still they're beautiful to these silly sons of bitches who have taken over the place. Fine a man for killing a cactus!"

He's rolling now and nothing will bank his fire.

"I don't see no reason for worshipping those goddamn cactus," he thunders. "You got this Saguaro National Monument if those fucking dudes want to go look at them. But in ranching country, they sure as hell need to be got rid of. So don't tell me nothing nice about cactus because I don't believe that."

But this country is no longer ranching country. It's no longer Buster Bailey country. In 1948, he won Best Mounted Cowboy at the Tucson Rodeo Parade. Now he lives in a dump without a horse, a steer, or an acre. The territory of his life is giving way under Pusch Ridge to factories, resort hotels, condominiums, and a real estate development peddled as wilderness estates.

The mountain itself plunges toward a future as an Alcatraz in an urban ocean. The big rock pile will be an island of wild things staring down the barrels of a city of straight, paved things.

Or maybe it is better to view the mountain as a queer kind of Noah's Ark loaded to the gunwales with species banished from the city below. Here lion and bighorn sheep and coatis and bear stare down at a restless army that has them under siege. But unlike Noah's Ark, there is no prophecy being offered that in forty days a dove will land on deck with a sprig alerting the inmates that this ocean of people is receding and freedom is at hand. This Ark may never unload. The real question is whether the ocean of human beings will rise and in a wave of energy wash over the range, crest and all.

The old man knows this. He knows his world has gone. He has but one claim on the present. He knew the mountain.

Buster Bailey has the Santa Catalina Mountains as a life. He pokes his finger on a map of the north slope and says, "This house down here where the park is, me and my dad built that in 1927, where the windmill is. That was the Bailey Ranch. It's had a hundred names since then. It's belonged to everyone in the country.

"I was the one who built that place up and lived with the millionaire woman from New York, stayed around her about ten years. I went in the service and she sold it. . . . So that place has changed hands many, many times.

"So that don't amount to much. That's all I can tell you." He stops telling and starts singing again:

I don't have much use for the women,
A true one will never be found.
They stay with a man while he's winning,
When he loses, they turn him down.

He winds down his song and smiles.

I started looking for the Santa Catalinas when I was seven years old and half a continent away in an earlier West called the Middle

West. The Illinois woods held a fresh carpet of snow, and I trailed a rabbit through the wet flakes. The oaks stood stripped of leaves, their thick trunks with a century of slow growth locked away in their rings.

It must have been a Saturday or Sunday—that's when the old man would flee the apartment in Chicago for a day in the country. His brother lived on ten acres of trees on a ridge above the Sag Canal. My uncle had ended up there after years working the Mississippi, sometimes on a government dredge, sometimes playing poker in the waterfront saloons. My mother's wedding ring had come from one of those games.

Now he had the trailer in the trees, no close neighbors, and a German shepherd that went for the throat of any visitors. While he and the old man talk away the winter afternoon, I wander off into the trees and cut the trail. I stumble along following the cottontail like I am on the sign of some fabled big foot. Near the small brook, I fall through the ice into the shallow water, struggle out and then push on. I quit when the tracks lead off into the bloom of a postwar subdivision.

Years later, my uncle did not like the hand he was dealt, picked up a pistol and backed away from all the games. I inherited the gun. And then another subdivision took his patch of woods. I don't know what happened to the dog.

By then I lived in Arizona and looked at the Catalinas and dreamed of cutting sign up there, of following the wild things. I kept seeking the sensation I felt on that winter day in the fresh snow when there were only two strands of tracks—mine and the beast's.

Today, the footing is bad and the cat's-claw rakes fine cuts across the arms. The north side of Pusch Ridge looks like a cake walk. Stroll an hour, maybe two, and the crest will be taken. But it does not work out that way.

The slopes run steep and a thick cover of agaves, cactus, mesquite, cat's-claw, and assorted shrubs make straight lines a dream.

The boot slips, with rock fragments always giving way and boulders demanding a hand-over-hand advance.

The mountain holds slabs a half billion years old and ridges punched up from the millions of years ago. They are islands in the spill of the rubble that has coursed down their slopes. The skirt is pretty much gneiss and the big forested dome in the center, Mt. Lemmon, is a bubble of granite.

For geologist Robert L. DuBois, the mountain sounds like this:

The core of the Santa Catalina Mountains is a granitic-gneissic complex, bounded on the north by a series of sedimentary rocks, part of which has been metamorphosed. The Oracle granite is exposed north of the sedimentary rock outcrops. Younger Precambrian, Paleozoic, and Cretaceous(?) sedimentary rocks are exposed along the east flank. Metasedimentary rocks crop out locally along the western and southwestern flanks. The ages of these gneissic and metasedimentary rocks and their relationship to rocks of known ages have been long a matter of discussion in southern Arizona.

The mountain stands as a monster example of what geographers call the basin and range province, a stretch of arid ground south of the Colorado Plateau characterized by lonely peaks awash in a desert sea of soils crumbled off their flanks. What these words mean is that you can walk from hot desert to the cool of a Douglas fir in a day, travel from Arizona to Canada in a few hours.

Clouds swirl across the cliff walls of the ridge, and on Lemmon five inches of snow have come for Thanksgiving Day. The deer season tempts a few hunters and every hour or two a shot pops across the canyons raking the north slopes. Buster Mountain dreams inside a cloud and then the white puff lifts and the peak tastes a brief flicker of sun.

There are no trails here. They have vanished with the cattle and Buster's old routes are memories the mountain has erased with a fresh burst of brush. We cut in off Sutherland Wash at the old Magee Ranch, now a few cement tanks and the roofless fingers of a rock house. Inside the ruin, naked women stare from the white-washed walls, visions sketched by adolescent hands in black paint. A lone window frames Table Mountain, the tower drifts in and out of the clouds surrounded by outlines of eager flesh and short messages of sexual desire.

We walk past and head up a draw that leads into the range. The sandy mouth soon narrows to a boulder choke and the forest of mesquite surrenders to hackberry and cat's-claw. The trees shake with cries and suddenly a great horned owl bolts from a limb and flies blind across the brush seeking shelter from the daylight.

We move at perhaps one mile an hour. It hardly matters. The mountains grow big when you step off a trail. A week before a hunter took a deer up a canyon near Buster's Spring and then spent two days packing the animal out.

As the drainage climbs and narrows, the stream comes to the surface in small rock-lined pools of clear water, ponds patrolled by insects flailing their tiny oars in the cold lenses of moisture. A bend shelters a juniper thriving in the cool pocket 500 feet below its normal world. Next comes an oak blocking the channel like a bouncer in a shot-and-a-beer joint.

We stop, eat a sandwich, and watch the cars run the highway down below. The purr of engines works across the slopes.

The modern environmental movement is a messianic mission to save wild ground and at its heart—at spots like this unnamed canyon where we sit on a rock and eat while a cold front beats against Pusch Ridge—it always seems to me that the center of the movement is a kind of empty barrel. The barrel at first looks full, in fact, overflowing with slogans, calendars, environmental impact statements, critical habitat lists, natural area plans, mitigation schemes, and big shovelfuls of tradeoffs. But after sorting through this barrel, I never find much that explains why I come to spots like this unnamed canyon. We have developed a new language of bureaucratic forms and categories and we wrap the wild ground in this gibberish. But we generally skirt the real issue. The way we live and work kills wild ground and when the wild ground is gone, we will vanish also.

Those of us who hunger for these places live as a kind of holding action, a group of marginal human beings huddled in the firestorm of energy called industrialism, people who retreat from time to time like ancient druids to this pagan ground that stamped us with our truest sense of self.

When I was a boy in Chicago, my father bought 200 acres of Wisconsin timber caught in a bend of the Black River. He'd spent a life riding the rails back and forth to his office on LaSalle Street and then one day he retired and disappeared. He showed up sitting at the kitchen table one gray Chicago day with a map of the property sketched on the flap of a pack of Zig Zag cigarette papers.

Like his brother, he had a trailer dragged onto the edge of his land, read books by kerosene light, and kept his beer cold in a refrigerator fueled by bottled gas. Miles of sandy ruts connected his domain to a country road. The trailer squatted on the bluff among the pine and oak, and down below stretched the swamp studded with huge cypress and tangled with a clawing web of vines.

The old man's father had been a lumberjack on this stretch of the Black River in the nineteenth century, and this particular parcel was one his axe had missed—possibly kept at bay by the swamp. My father did not know words like "environmentalist" and he hated rules. Although Aldo Leopold had spent long years in patches of Wisconsin just like this, my father did not know him and may not have cared for his message.

Ruin near Table Mountain

He kept a loose camp and pitched his trash right down the hill to rust and rot among the trees. He did not hunt. Neither did he fish. He knew no flowers and did not listen to the birds.

One fall day, he sat there drinking a Blatz and chewing on some Shakespeare when the sound of a chainsaw rent the air. The old man lifted off his chair like a bird of prey and stormed into his forest where he found a neighboring farmer cutting a little firewood.

He ran him off. He turned a deaf ear to all the offers of timbering a slice of his woods for a share of the take. The local men told him the trees would hardly be missed, that his woods would look the same when they had finished culling them.

He would not budge.

He did not explain these matters.

He presented them to me as a kind of gruff riddle and left me to my own answers. He would sit at the kitchen table smoking a rolled cigarette. The fingers were stained with nicotine, the eyes sharp like the edge of a stiletto. He did not speak of his forest. Nor did he choose to go into town.

I am nine, ten, eleven, twelve, and I watch the old man read. I hunt. I fish. I ramble. He ignores me. He seems blind to the land, yet he refuses to cut or knick or gouge or mark it.

For a privy, he digs a hole in the ground, cuts the seat out of a chair, and is done. For a bed, he lashes some logs together out under the pines and nails a tarp across the expanse.

Friends come up from the city to hunt and fish. The old man says nothing. He neither objects nor joins in. He reads, he broods, and decades later I snap to attention on a big rock in the Santa Catalina Mountains and feel his breath upon my neck, his message floating through my mind like a soft, relentless sound. A long time ago, Aldo Leopold argued we must learn to think like a mountain. This we have not done. Our trail guides prove useless for such a task.

I stumble upon random clues. The Maricopas are a bunch of Indians that now hang on near the sprawl of Phoenix about one hundred miles to the north. Ralph Cameron is one of them and like us he spent most of his life as an exile from places like the canyon under Pusch Ridge. In his case, he did his time in a Los Angeles steel factory. Ralph Cameron, in a recent anthology of Indian writing, *Spirit Mountain*, says this:

> *When I was young, I saw my land as I grew up.*
> *The rivers were many and without price.*
> *The mountains there had not been touched.*
> *They were beautiful, tall and big and they stood out.*
> *The land I was born on was clean.*
> *The rain washed it and purified it.*
> *You saw it and it was very good.*
> *Now it is not like that.*
> *I see this.*
> *This is my tradition.*
> *A tree half fallen down with its roots showing—I feel*
> *I am like that, I say we will stand again.*
> *I see many things are left that haven't vanished yet. . . .*
> *The people will walk again, I say.*
> *We will again have the truth.*

Lunch is over and we head down and out. I am not an Indian and I cannot think like a mountain. Overhead a redtail hawk screams and I stare through binoculars and think of it simply as a big bird.

I am eight or nine years old and I walk into the storefront branch of the Chicago Public Library on 79th Street. There are very few books—the city that works has little use for the printed word. I have seen these things: carp jumping in Illinois creeks; a water moccasin being beaten to death by a black man with a cane pole; the hard, cool desert of northeast Mexico; the core of Yellowstone beckoning with elk and moose on a July day.

I open a green book on big game. The page flames with a line drawing of a moose half hidden in the tules of a bog. Outside the library window, traffic crawls down 79th Street under a gray Chicago sky. In my hand, the moose feeds and there is no sound and no sign of city.

I have spent my life trying to cross from that street into that page, trying to escape into that bog. I do not speak to Buster Bailey about the moose sighted in a library book on 79th Street, about the rabbit trailed through the fresh snow of an Illinois woods. I do not speak much at all, but simply listen hour by hour. And what he tells me through songs, quips, snorts, bellers, sighs, and tales is how he came to bond with that big mountain.

He's 110 feet down a hand-dug well at Rancho Vistosa and it is the tail end of the 1920s. Just to the south, the Catalinas furl a rocky brow and the ranch sits hard by the sweep of Cañada del Oro where it crosses Oracle Highway. Buster is in the prime of his life. He shovels a load of dirt and then signals two Mexicans up on top to haul it away in the bucket hooked to a windlass. As he waits, he huddles in a steel culvert, a kind of instant shelter at the bottom of the big hole.

Then things go bad. The walls start to give way, the dirt pours over him, and Buster Bailey, the barbed wire man, the maintenance man, the well man, is buried alive. He jerks the rope, he shouts, but the men on the surface don't sense the problem.

Finally, the cave-in telegraphs its force to the top and the men start cranking up the lift.

"My shirt was full of dirt," he recalls a half century later, "my pockets were full of dirt. I couldn't breathe when I got to the top of the hole. Of course I coughed up dirt and shit out of my lungs. Sat around there dizzy for a while." The old man pauses and savors this ancient hurt.

"That goddamn near ruined me right there," he snorts, "and hell that was in 1929. I was lucky to be alive and this old boy said, 'you must have a rabbit's foot to come through that.'"

Buster Bailey

The land now looks so innocent of cow country danger. Rancho Vistosa, with its pink walls and trees and quiet air in the bend of the Cañada del Oro, poises on the brink of becoming a subdivision. The cows have mostly gone away and the cowboys huddle in urban saloons acting out a costume drama. This part of the big mountain is just about dead—the time of the branding iron, lasso, men on horseback crashing through the claws of the mimosa chasing stag steers. But it still throbs like a beating heart in Buster Bailey's memories.

Buster's got a television he salvaged from the dump and the machine tells him that his world has vanished.

"Turn on the TV," he roars, "and what'll you see? They're either fucking or killing and I can't stand it. The day of my kind of people is gone, mister. It's not the same kind of people anymore."

He stares off into space for a minute, his eyes wandering out the door to work over the towers of Pusch Ridge, and then he snaps back and asks if anybody's heard the story of the Two Great Hurts. Buster's had his share of hurting and as he launches into the tale, the words seem to create a bridge into that other world, the time of working men and cow country.

There was this cowboy up on the range in Montana, he begins with a smile, and he went into a dentist's office to have all his teeth pulled. The dentist said, "Well, let me deaden'm first." The cowboy said, "Don't need no deader. I've had two great hurts in my life and this will be nothing."

So the doctor rips out all his teeth and stands amazed when the cowboy never flinches. Finally, he asks, "Just what were these two great hurts that prepared you for tooth extraction without any deadener?"

"Well," the cowboy says, "I got up one morning and went out to check the stock and the wind whipped across the snow in the twenty below air. Just as soon as I felt the blast, my bowels started to tighten up and I had to relieve myself.

"I squatted down out there and the stuff hit the ground and landed right on the pan of a bear trap buried under the snow. The big jagged jaws of the trap went snap! right on my private parts."

"That," he allows, "was the first great hurt."

"My God!" exclaims the doctor. "If that was the first great hurt, what was the second?"

The cowboy looks him in the eye and explains with an even tone, "When I hit the end of that six foot chain."

The adventure in the well was one of Buster's three great hurts. They all came as part of the package, working the mountain and the bajadas—those alluvial fans spilling off the slopes.

Buster fingers the map where his family settled on the Cañada del Oro and reflects, "I come damn near getting killed three times within a quarter mile."

He and two Mexican guys were fencing up on the bajada near some Indian ruins. Old village sites stud the first bench of land off the big wash, Hohokam relics left from the time of Christ and all those centuries tumbling into what scholars call the Middle Ages. Circles of rock mark the pit houses. Strange walls snake across the land. Archaeologists have been busy digging these places to grab a last clue before the houses and factories bury them for a good long time.

Well, Buster and his friends were putting in that fence and he rammed his steel bar into the earth and heard a crunch. He peered down and found a tin can and inside the can was a passel of dynamite caps left by some old prospector.

Buster turned to his pals and told them they'd all come within an eyelash of being blown to kingdom come. They looked at the innocent little caps and did not believe him. He considered their disbelief for a moment. When the caps blew, boulders flew like popcorn and a giant hole opened up in the ground.

The third great hurt nipped a little more deeply into Buster. His dad took to the notion of opening a gas station right after the family arrived in the late twenties, and he set his boy to hauling dirt off the bajada to fill in the roadside site. Buster had a ton-and-a-half Model T truck, an exception in his lifelong love of Chevies.

He'd thunder up on the ridge, toss a couple of tons of soil in the rig, and then come down in the overloaded machine, hobbling over the rough ground.

"I put about three tons on that little son of a bitch," he smiles, "and those Ford trucks in those days would rear up. So I got about halfway down when it rared up and it went off into that canyon and turned me over five times, me and those soft chollas in there.

"When that son of a bitch quit rolling the cab top was mashed down on me and the old glass was all over in there with me and all I had was a knick." Except for those soft chollas.

God, Buster hates cactus, hates them with a fire pure and clean, despises them like a Christian facing Satan, wants them killed, slaughtered, axed, burned, punished, hacked, chopped, and tortured. Wants them gone. He got this passion the day he hauled dirt down from the bajada for his dad's gas station.

"There were more chollas in me," he winces, "than you ever saw in your life. Them sons of bitches really hurt here in the upper lip."

He got a hack saw and cut the cab off the truck and then he got the thing righted and put the front tires back on and worried the machine out of the canyon. Then he went home. "They poured water on me," he intones, "and pulled cholla out of me. By God, everytime I went to bed for six months—the chollas you'll find in your legs when you get next to your bed blanket."

So it is a different kind of mountain for Buster. The rocks and slopes and bulges of land call forth a repertoire of hard times, good times, old times. He can look at a patch of mesquite and spin right back to a place of more cows than people.

It is the fall of 1984 and in one day a bulldozer has mowed down every mesquite lining the south side of the Oracle Highway for a mile. The road needs widening and the giant old trees now lie as heaps of trash along the pavement leading to Buster's old ranch.

"These smart people," he begins as the green slaughterhouse slaps him in the face, "want to poison the mesquite today. They don't want'm to live. If you're going to be an Arizonian, mesquite's been one of the most valuable things in the country since the year one. The Indians made just about everything they could eat out of that.

"Then they holler about this broiled mesquite steak over a mesquite fire. All the crying they do over it and then they want to poison them. How stupid can you get. And then you call me crazy because I don't like this modern crap they got going."

His eyes get crystal clear now and flame blue at the thought of murdered mesquite.

"In the old days," he explains, "that was all the posts you had. You cut all your fence posts out of these washes. I've cut thousands and thousands of them up out of these washes. At Rancho Vistosa, I used to get up and cut twenty-five posts before breakfast and I'm talkin' about big ones, not little pecker posts. I've built miles and miles and miles of fence."

It's a Sunday and groups of people scavenge the heaps of bulldozed mesquite. Families work with chain saws and stack cords as the old groves of trees surrender to one last hurrah of firewood.

Buster looks at the mountains and shifts to teaching the old geography, one that has slightly different notes from the modern hiking maps. The first gouge to the west he calls Alamo Canyon because there used to be a big cottonwood up there. Then comes Cement Tank because they put a trough in there. After that is Dead Horse for a dead horse found one day. Then Montrose on whose upper reaches Buster Spring bubbles away. And over the ridge from that is Romero for the old ranching family that came into the country in the nineteenth century. When Buster arrived in the 1920s, they were still here, still ranching. And they became his neighbors.

Everything comes tumbling back. In the late twenties, he went to cowboying up at the Willow Springs place ten, fifteen miles to the north, a ranch sprawling under the gaze of the mountain. A bunch of Oklahoma Indians, oil rich ones, owned the spread, and Buster recalls that time with a sigh.

"Every whore and slut in Tucson," he says, "came out there. You may think you can't get sick of that stuff but you do after wallowing in it a while."

The thirties landed like a hammer on ranch country. "It was during the Depression," he explains, "and you couldn't buy a job. I've worked hard for a dollar a day." Finally, he turned to bootlegging, a thing he still recalls with a mixture of pride in his product and a kind of caution over the reputation that hangs around that kind of work.

He swings his hand over the north face of the mountain and says, "You go up and down those canyons and you'll find parts of stills in every one of them."

He made his 100 proof white lightning and peddled it through Steinfeld's fancy grocery in Tucson. They kept the stuff in plain crocks in the walk-in cooler. He used charred oak barrels—essential he feels for a decent product—cracked corn, sugar, and yeast. When the weather was warm, three days made whiskey. When the chill days came, maybe five days were required.

After Prohibition ended, he quit the bootlegging until the Second World War plopped him down in New Guinea. The Captain came around and expressed alarm over the way the boys were guzzling any kind of industrial fluid they could find in their search for a jungle high. He put Buster to work, and soon he had copper coil, barrels (rescued from the dump where they'd landed as discarded Coke containers), corn meal, and the works. Buster whipped out his white lightning in sixty-five-gallon batches and after that he could hardly get a decent night's sleep what with the troops singing until dawn.

Foothills development

He served three years and twenty-seven days, and when he got back the mountain was still there, but the millionaire gal was gone and so was his land. But that's a different story.

"I don't know," he suddenly snaps, "why they should sacrifice the country for these goddamn backpackers."

He shuffles across his one-room home and fetches an old Army ammo box. The lid says: THIS BOX TAKEN FROM A WRECKED ARMY JEEP ON BATTLEFIELD NEAR HOLLANDIA, NEW GUINEA. Ancient photographs come tumbling out. Buster with a nephew at the corral of the old spread. Buster standing by a big log up in the ponderosa of Mt. Lemmon. Favorite horses pose with their front legs on a cement block. He rips one from the pile and proudly shows off Baby, the best horse he ever had.

Some people find it peculiar to talk to a horse but Buster never had that problem. He knew and the horses knew. Baby understood everything. She'd walk into the general store on Mt. Lemmon, filch a soda pop and drink it.

There she stands with Buster on the porch of the old store. They both look happy and the photograph comes from a time and place that must have ended a thousand years ago.

He looks out at the booming city and says, "I don't know about growth. It sure won't be good whatever it is."

THE LAST RESORT

The temperature of these mountain slopes seldom exceeds 80 degrees in summer, and they are continually fanned by refreshing breezes. The region is an attractive one as a summer resort. When adequate accommodations can be secured, there is no doubt that this region will be largely resorted to by the ladies of Tucson who seek to escape the tropical climate of our heated term.

Wherever the ladies go the gentlemen will follow and thus an attractive society will be gathered and the expense of long and tedious trips to distant states will be avoided. Already the attractions of this delightful region are being availed by some of our health seeking families.

ARIZONA WEEKLY STAR, AUGUST 18, 1881

An Abert's squirrel slips down the ponderosa trunk on New Year's Eve. Sabino Creek roars between banks of snow and Summerhaven seems to doze in the afternoon sun. The two real estate offices in town are closed for the day as well as the gift shop, and signs up and down the road advertise cabins for rent, houses for rent.

On the hills, children shout as their toboggans glide down the slopes. A few dogs wander around, and here and there a resident strolls down the road to check the mail or take an airing.

For about a century, some people have been expecting great things of this site, a pine forest next to a desert city. The great things have yet to happen.

Summerhaven harbors a few hundred cabins on federal and deeded land, almost no work, a long commute to Tucson, and a sewage problem that grows more intricate each year and is never resolved.

The thing people have dreamed of, the big money, has yet to arrive. Down the road a little from the village center is The Retreat. In July 1984, The Retreat advertised itself this way: "For the select few. A few very select homes. Think of it."

The developers promised twenty-eight resort homes wedged into five-and-a-quarter acres of private land, each house running 1,800 square feet and costing $175,000. There would be a clubhouse, jacuzzi, sun deck, and open air cafe. By late 1984, the few had not shown up and The Retreat was in a dormant phase.

Such schemes are recurrent on the mountain. In 1975, one investor plotted a lodge and restaurant for weekend visitors.

"It's time Mount Lemmon," the man counseled, "be brought out of the Dark Ages with some twentieth-century accommodations." Nothing came of this venture either.

There have been changes on the mountaintop. In 1915, Forrest Shreve, the great botanist of the Sonoran Desert, wrote:

Whatever may have been the original form of the Santa Catalinas they have been so far worked upon by erosion and weathering that they now possess almost no relatively level areas. . . . On the summit of Mount Lemmon there is a nearly level area of at least 100 acres. . . . This restricted area of nearly level land is a last relic of a portion of the original structural form of the mountain, and it will not be many centuries until it is reduced to the narrow form of the lower ridges.

Shreve guessed wrong. The top was wiped out in the 1950s and not by erosion, but by bulldozers hacking out a site for an Air Force Radar station, now a memento of the Cold War reborn as a university laboratory.

I stand in front of the village post office and look at the ruins of Zimmerman's store, a building burned down in the early 1970s.

This is a decades-old human community, and it has a lot of memories. I've got a few myself.

My old man took great pride in his red truck. The machine was designed to be a bread van or to deliver things in the city. He did not use it that way.

He put in a stove, gas lights, curtains, and a bed. The bed revealed a lot of thinking. He liked to drink Blatz in long-necked bottles, and he built his bunk exactly one Blatz high so that he could store a row of the cases right underneath.

When I was sixteen, I took a job on the mountain helping out as a kind of Gunga Din on an ecological survey of the range. Each morning we would hike into a portion of the mountain, run out tape, and take a census of plant populations along this imaginary line. I had to learn hundreds of species and live in Summerhaven.

The old man loaned me his truck for the job and I parked it right next to Zimmerman's store.

The two scientists were from the East and lived with their wives in cabins. They found the mountain a spare place to dwell and had the *New York Times* delivered weekly to fortify themselves. Their wives seemed bored by big peaks, and one of them spent each day reading Sherlock Holmes.

This did not seem an unusual air in Summerhaven. The small village was filled with people who had come up to escape the pressures of the city. They would walk down to Zimmerman's store, go over their mail, and sit on their porches. But they did not seem at peace with the place. There was nothing to do but walk the mountain, and the mountain was steep and hard.

Once a week, I would eat in the lodge down the road and sit in the dining room alone. I always had a blueberry cobbler for dessert and played a piece on the jukebox by the Ramsey Lewis Trio.

At night, I would light the gas lantern in the van and pore over botany books.

One day at the lodge I met a woman about thirty who lived on the mountain. She said her husband worked down below and only came up for the weekends. She seemed a very tense woman, her mouth a hard line and her eyes small and tight with something I could not understand in my adolescence. She invited me to come by for drinks.

When I entered the cabin, her Indian maid scurried from the room to get the cocktails. We sat down on chairs. I was very young and nervous and all I could think of was her husband, some huge man wielding a machete and a gun who would crash through the screen door.

The woman sat on her chair across from me and tried to make conversation. I stumbled in my speech and when the drinks came, I nervously clinked the ice in the glass. Outside the ponderosas were big black shafts against the night sky.

She said, "I am not trying to seduce you."

After a while, I bolted and I remember her sitting there on a chair, body upright and rigid, in the nice cabin on the mountain. The Indian woman stood at the edge of the room and the place seemed empty of everything but this tension I could taste but not name.

Now I'm a lot older and so is Summerhaven. I walk into the Alpine Lodge for a quiet brunch. The bar is empty. Two video games (Pac Man and Centipede) await players.

Everyone wants a cabin in the mountains. The cabin will be log, the fireplace stone, and outside the door, pines whisper with the breeze. In the spring, birds eat bread crumbs from the windowsill and the wildflowers line the path to the stream. At dusk you sit on the porch in a rocking chair and watch the forest go dark. Every now and then, a deer, always a doe, sometimes with a fawn, browses in the glen just down from the cabin. The deer shows no fear at your presence. You both belong here and feel a deep peace.

In the winter, you come up with a friend for the holidays. The windows frost at the edges and frame a view of pine and fir towering over snow-covered hills. On Christmas Eve, you build a big fire, and a tree nicely trimmed stands in the corner. You drink eggnog and listen to the logs crackle and feel the touch of something you sense is basically American, old, and true. At midnight you both go out on the porch and shiver for a moment in the cold air. A full moon hunts through the pines and you sip twelve-year-old scotch.

Everybody wants a cabin in the mountains, and Summerhaven is a registry of this dream's changing fashions over the last ten decades. In recent years, the idea is being questioned and the Forest Service makes noises of ending leases previously granted, choking back private holdings, and limiting growth. But everyone still wants that cabin.

In the cafe, three men sit at a corner table. They talk numbers. This is another part of the dreams for the mountaintop: the main chance.

One intones, "$1391.20 equals $2782.40 equals. . . ."

A second man scribbles these figures down as fast as they spew from a pocket calculator. The third man simply beams.

The two men running the tally are dressed in flannel shirts, work pants, and boots. The third man wears an apron. Finally, the numbers push past $11 million. The men pause at this figure.

"Double your money?" one asks.

The second man advises, "The only way you can catch that kind of action is the Kentucky Derby . . . and know exactly how the race will come out."

The three ponder this possibility—the sheer magic in the idea of pegging each horse correctly, of laying off enough bets around the country, of making the big score. The old year is ticking away and this notion makes the future look like a good place to be.

The man with the apron is the key to the whole matter. He can see the race. He can read the horses. He knows the answer. But it must be the year after next. This point is essential.

His friends ask him why. Why must they wait two years to cash in on his ability to see the race finish?

He cannot explain the matter but they accept his words and settle in for the wait. Music pours softly from speakers in the cafe. Linda Ronstadt asks, "What's New?"

I have come to my cabin in the woods. It is 1968 and when I think of the Catalinas, they merely offer some fragrance of home and a rock pile I take for granted and barely know. The two-room cabin sits on the lip of the hill and catches the murmur of a river in northern Wisconsin. I drink a can of Heileman's Old Style and listen to the wind rustle the trees. The pale green table nestles against the kitchen window. I can sit, soak up the sun coming through the panes, feel the cool beads of the moisture on the can of beer, and hear the river voices. This year the big news comes from the war in Asia. Here in this timbered-out region of the upper Great Lakes, there has been no big news for over half a century.

I am always late. As a boy, I find Yellowstone a century and a half after John Coulter reveled in its geysers, wild beasts, and space. I first see the plains eighty years after the bison have been freighted off by trains to the boneyards of the East. My family stops at a roadside cafe in Wyoming and I eat a buffalo burger, visit Cody, and touch a doorknob at Buffalo Bill's Hotel Irma. At twelve, I discover the Southwest with Indians tame, bad men sleeping in Boot Hill, roads conquering the peaks, and the flats a crazy quilt of empty streets begging for speculators to make them subdivisions. This quiet cabin by the river is one more place for me to be late. This time I am six decades after the sunset of this land.

The old woman stays up in the house. She has survived eighty winters or more and now at the tail end of the 1960s, she still savors the last run down the river. In her home, hooked rugs dot the hardwood floors, and the light walls display cabinets with glass doors. Everything feels cool to the touch, and the sun falls through the windows with the limp force of the north.

The town has been over for a long time, and the woman hangs on with her cabins by the river, a kind of relic of the boom days. Fishermen come to throw blood baits for the big channel cats slumbering on the bottom, and she gets by with this trade. This is the cutover region, the upper third of Wisconsin, Michigan, and Minnesota, and people here have mastered the art of getting by.

She speaks brightly—she is a cheerful woman—and shows her trophies, case after case of Indian buckskin decorated with rows of colored beads. The work was fashioned before the last drive, things gathered in by her father in the final harvest of the forest and the forest people. She senses the value of the old things and clings to them tenaciously as a link with the time when the north lived in a constant spring.

In 1847, Frederick Graham, a young Englishman, cruised the Great Lakes forest and scribbled, "Trees, trees, trees for everlasting. . . . I shall hate the sight of wood for the future."

In 1852, Congressman Ben Eastman of Wisconsin stood on the floor of the House of Representatives in Washington, D.C., and boasted, "Upon the rivers which are tributary to the Mississippi and also upon those which empty themselves into Lake Michigan, there are interminable forests of pine, sufficient to supply the wants of the citizens . . . for all time to come."

In the 1890s, Lincoln Steffens, soon to be a famous muckraker, but then a young reporter, cornered Frederick Weyerhaeuser in his St. Paul office and had an off-the-record interview with the timber baron.

Steffens wondered what the toll had been on the great man for his part in cutting flat the monster forest of the Upper Midwest.

"What did it cost you?" Steffens finally asked.

Weyerhaeuser clearly understood the question, but he said only that he had "often wanted to talk it over with somebody."

The old woman does not concern herself with these matters. She lives as a prisoner of them but does not speak of the old carnage.

In 1890, the Upper Midwest produced thirty-five percent (by value) of the nation's lumber products. By 1920, this had slipped to eight percent, and by 1940, to four percent. For two hundred years, from the 1530s to the 1730s, Europeans traversing the great forest made almost no mention of the endless green expanse, a kind of Amazon of the north. The trees seemed incidental to trappers seeking furs, explorers searching for that Northwest Passage, or to priests hungry for a harvest of souls. Then for a brief moment between 1870 and 1920, saws bit deeply into the north. And suddenly it was over.

The place was cut flat. The last run of logs past the old woman's place was in 1905 or 1906. A handful of men, trapped by the river's power, rode the rafts of trees over the falls to their deaths. The woods fell still.

The Santa Catalina Mountains that I know were spared because of places like Jim Falls. What happened in this flat glacial pan of trees, trees, and more trees helped to create an urge to conserve the forests, and the urge resulted in laws that became shields for ranges all over the West.

The story is very simple. In Wisconsin, for example, the governor in 1856 asked the federal government to sell off the timberlands to private interests. He argued they would take better care of the forests. From time to time, commissions and studies questioned the cutting of the trees. Such voices were ignored and the studies shelved. As late as the time of World War I, a movement to set aside state reserves in Wisconsin met with an uproar by citizens of the north who argued such a move would cause the "rejunglizing" of their counties.

By the first decade it was largely over—a swath from Michigan through Minnesota had been cut almost completely to the ground. There was bramble, second-growth timber, a dense wall of green, but the huge trees, the legendary white pines of enormous girth, were gone and not to be seen again. When I was in college in the late sixties, I would canoe the rivers of northern Wisconsin and every once in a while at some impossible rock-ribbed bend of the channel, a glen of a few acres would appear with gigantic trees. This was all Wisconsin had left of the big forest that greeted the first Europeans.

"Why do you want to be a forester, boy?" one old lumberjack asked a young man in the 1930s. "We cut all the pines!"

From this great sea of stumps and others pocking the eastern United States came the stimulus for the creation of federal forest reserves in 1891, the creation of the U.S. Forest Service in 1905, and the effort to save places like the Santa Catalina Mountains which were set aside by the scratch of a pen on July 2, 1902. And out of the jumble of laws came the legal loopholes that resulted in places like Summerhaven, towns wrangled from legislation originally enacted for trees, not subdividers.

The cutover region fed a cause that sought to make the West an example of conservation, forest management, range management, and a host of programs the federal government stamped on the land. Gifford Pinchot, a man of Yale, headed the new organization and his life became a crusade. It is 1906 and he awaits an early morning train in Tucson. To kill time, he visits scientist D. T. McDougal at the new Carnegie Desert Laboratory atop Tumamoc Hill, the home base for botanist Forrest Shreve. McDougal and Pinchot spend the night designing a new uniform for the rangers.

All this energy is triggered in part by what took place in the Jim Falls of the Midwest. To stroll in this small village is to visit one of the sources of a new religion.

I walk out of the old woman's house. The walls are white clapboard and look very clean in the spring light. I go to the center of the village a few blocks away. Men sit and drink coffee in the small cafe. They are local farmers trying to find a living in the scattered fields carved out of the sea of stumps left by the great cutting. The room is cigarette smoke and languor. For several decades, this was the center of the earth's hunger for wood, as important in some ways to nineteenth-century man as the Middle East is to our civilization. Now it is a forgotten battlefield, a Gettysburg with the fallen buried and the war tales left to the dead. People drive through, stop and fish, take a cabin and look over the woods, and never imagine the great forest is actually a great cemetery.

Up at the old house, the woman moves about among her Indian treasures. The buckskin rots with age. The people who made such things have become barely a memory. The Midwest is a warehouse of lessons no one pays much attention to. Here the forces of my culture once gathered, feasted, and then pushed on.

The cabin at Jim Falls is very peaceful. Almost nothing happens in the immediate neighborhood. In the evening the fishermen emerge from their cabins and go down to the river to throw their blood baits. You can sit there and drink beer after beer and listen to the mosquitoes humming through the screens. On the dark river, lanterns glow where men huddle and wait for the big bottom fish to open their jaws and swallow the hook.

I am very far from home but I drink and sit on ground zero of the very thing that touched the Santa Catalinas of my dreams.

I do not know this in 1968. I just feel the laziness in the air and sense that something big and hungry fed on these woods and then moved on.

In the morning, there are these huge catfish, gray bodies glistening and long whiskers framing the mouth, lying about in tubs with their bellies slit where they have been gutted.

By day the fishermen sleep. In the afternoon, they get up and move about, talk about their fishing, and brag of the numbers they will snare that coming night.

They are very cheerful and are here on a holiday from their jobs in the city or on farms to the south. They have these cabins, rented to be sure, but still their cabins and the whole experience feels good to them. The dream is very old, and anyone born and reared in this country feels the tug of the dream. So they enjoy themselves and fish and speak of more fishing. To hear them talk, you would think there was no tomorrow.

When John Lemmon and his wife arrived on the top ridge of the Catalinas in 1881, their guide, Emerson Oliver Stratton, led them to a cabin near what would become Summerhaven and found two men busy cutting trees. The next morning Stratton got up and shot seven deer.

In 1882, under the Timber Homestead Act, Frank Webber homesteaded 160 acres at the site. There was no road to the top then and no way to get lumber to market. The filing was perhaps a fraud—a common practice in that era. All over the West, the new federal laws, those beginning to emerge as people slowly grasped the devastation of the Upper Midwest and the East, were considered a nuisance and blithely ignored or gotten around.

Webber tried to make a go of the place, hauled logs with oxen, and later built cabins at the junction of Carter and Sabino canyons. Others were speculating on the resort future of the mountain. Down on Oracle Ridge at the Apache Mine, cottages were built in 1882 in the hope that "Tucson excursionists" would fill them in the summer months. The Webber homestead was later abandoned, and then in 1912 the land was patented.

By 1918, Jim Westfalls was running a sawmill and had built the Mariposa Hotel. The year before in 1917, the old Webber homestead finally came to full flower. The statute of limitations had expired for fraud, and instantly the 160-acre plot was subdivided with twenty homes scheduled to be built.

Summer cabins had been in the air for several years. The Forest Supervisors received fifty inquiries for leases in 1916 and figured that the mountain could host maybe five hundred cabins. Lease terms in 1918 were $25 a year for a five-acre plot and a maximum lease of thirty years.

With 1920 and the finishing of a dirt road up the back side, Summerhaven enjoyed a small boom. Several houses went up at once. By 1930, the lease for 1.5 acres was $15 per year and around 1935, fifty-seven out of ninety-five lots (50 by 106 feet) were filled. The thing sputtered along: fifty new homes in Willow Canyon in 1948; sixty lots at Loma Linda.

Tony Zimmerman arrives in 1943. He had been teaching school in Tucson and retired to the mountain. He builds the Mount Lemmon Inn, operates a small sawmill, and becomes a leading figure in the community.

Old habits die hard on the mountain. In 1947, Randolph Jenks files a mining claim near Summerhaven and begins subdividing it. The matter goes to court and Jenks eventually has to return 148 acres but gets to keep a patch, and private land at Summerhaven jumps from 160 acres to 270. In 1955, the Multiple Use Mining Law is passed to end such land acquisitions.

By the late 1960s, the Forest Service reconsiders having a human community in a reserve of trees, streams, and animals. The old newspaper clippings are filled with debate about the village. Sabino Creek has become an open sore as the population overwhelms the capacity of septic tanks. Pima County puts in a sewage system but overflows still persist. The Forest Service buys back 65 acres, and Summerhaven is cut to a private base of 205 acres.

The town enters a bitter era of plans and counter plans. Some want the place to grow and some want it to shrink. Summerhaven and the mountain have survived into a new world. Where once the mountain was lumber, gold, and the chimera of summer resorts, now it has slowly become something called nature. The process required decades.

There are idle hints of this new idea in Tucson during the 1920s. The local nature society in 1925 hosts a Saturday afternoon picnic in Sabino Canyon where a Professor V. L. Ayres speaks of the antiquity of the range's rocks and J. F. Breazeale of the U.S. Bureau of Plant Industry takes the group to a petroglyph recently discovered. Mr. Breazeale reckons the stone scratching looks like a Maltese cross with two arrows and notes it is similar to drawings found in caves in the Pyrenees Mountains and other parts of Europe. The visitors have supper and then Mrs. C. N. Catlin recites an original poem, "Ode to a Skunk," which the local paper says "commemorates a pathetic incident which took place on Mount Lemmon last summer. . . ."

A leader in this new way of looking at the mountain is Arizona legislator F. E. A. Kimball. In 1926, he laments in the *Tucson Citizen* that "it is probable that were the Catalina mountain range several hundred miles away from Tucson more local people would be familiar with its charms as a recreational resort than at present, as it seems a universal fact that 'distance lends enchantment.'"

He points out that wild turkeys will soon be restocked on the mountain and that thankfully the deer were protected before total extermination was possible. Kimball is a state leader in protecting wildlife.

Two years later, the Santa Catalina natural area is dedicated, a 4,464-acre reserve on the crest near Marshall Gulch and forty people watch five reels of conservation films at the Mariposa Lodge. The natural area is the first of its kind designated by the Forest Service and F. E. A. Kimball is the man who got it done. G. A. Pearson, director of the Southwest Forest Experiment Laboratory in Flagstaff, gives a talk and sounds a new message:

By virtue of its location [the Natural Area] at the summit of a high mountain, difficult of access for purposes of exploitation, the Santa Catalina area approaches more nearly the primeval state than most forest areas in the Southwest. . . . Obviously, the area should be closed to all forms of commercial use and human occupancy. . . . Human interference must be restricted to a minimum. Man's impulse to exterminate predatory animals, for example, must be curbed.

In 1930, Kimball is dead and local people name a peak in the front range Mount Kimball in his memory.

But within this movement to save the mountain in the name of Nature, there is another drive, one pushed by Kimball himself. Originally, trails laced the Catalinas, either remnants from the paths of the Indians or new ones cut by the Forest Service in order to police the mountain for fires. In 1920, the back road from Oracle to Mount Lemmon is finished and automobiles arrive. But this drive takes three-and-a-half hours and many are not yet satisfied.

Kimball sounds the battle cry in his newspaper article of 1926: he wants a road up the front side facing the city. The route he pushes will go up Sabino Canyon to Soldier's Camp on the crest. The federal government has already paid $15,000 for a survey. Kimball argues that Tucson spends $50,000 a year on firewood and that the road will pay for itself in no time with cords of wood for heating the city.

And he does not forget recreation:

The road would also result in a marvelous saving of money now expended outside of Arizona by Tucson residents as the new road would cause thousands of local people to spend their vacations in the Catalinas where they now go east and to California. With three to five feet of snow covering the Catalinas from January first to April first of each year it could be utilized for winter sports now so popular in the east. A road on the south side would land one by automobile within a few rods of this winter paradise. . . .

His notion becomes local crusade pushed by the *Tucson Citizen*. When critics argue the mountain lacks abundant water, the newspaper crackles with stories listing babbling brooks and certain springs. Editorials extol roads gouging mountains near other western cities, and by 1930 local boosters have opened a downtown office to push for the road. The windows of the storefront are decorated with pine cones.

The county Board of Supervisors passes a resolution in 1931 advocating the highway, "not only providing a travel route over the mountains of remarkable scenic grandeur, but also making readily accessible extensive recreational areas and numerous sites for the building of summer homes."

The federal government finally coughs up the cash ($1,250,000) for the route in 1933 and originally plans to cut a road up the front and down the back. The back side never gets paved and the work on the front takes longer than expected. Convicts build the highway.

The first federal prison camp on the mountain opened under Bigelow Peak in June 1933, and the inmates lived in tents. The first winter drove them down to the valley floor on the Tucson side. By 1939, the new highway is six miles up at Molino Basin, and the convicts are spending too much time commuting each day to the work site.

So a new prison camp is built just above Molino and a water witch, Ralph Augustus Wetmore, finds good water after drilling for forty-five days through solid granite. He uses a mesquite fork to locate the well. The convicts toil on and finish the thing in 1950 (the prison camp lingers as a federal youth camp until 1972).

The road is an idea almost beyond reproach. As pioneer naturalist Kimball noted, it puts the mountain within a few rods of the automobile. Even before the road in the 1930s, the mountain blooms with summer camps for children and dudes. The Boy Scouts first arrive at Bear Wallow in 1914, and by 1933 forest rangers are troubled by their frisky use of little hatchets and their mania for building campfires.

The image of the mountain feeds new tourist hungers, and the road helps to sell the place. One outfitter pitches the thing this way:

SEE THE CATALINAS FIRST

"ENJOY THE WEST IN A WESTERN WAY"

You may have admired the grandeur of the Santa Catalina Mountains from the highway, but you will never appreciate the scenic beauty of this range until you get astride of a surefooted pony. . . . On return the party may group around a regular old fashioned chuck wagon and enjoy supper, cowboy fashion, by the light of the open camp fire.

A brochure for Summerhaven in the 1930s states, "You want rest and relaxation in the open away from the noise and confusion of the city. You long for the pine clad mountains where the air is fresh and the water cold and pure. Summerhaven is the answer."

But there is another voice, buried alive for almost half a century, that questioned such things. He lives in Wisconsin by the time the highway is blasted up the front side, but much earlier, when he was a young man, he came here to the Santa Catalina Mountains.

He favored a cabin by the Wisconsin River and in the summer of 1948, he died fighting a brush fire near his retreat. He left the draft of a book that was published two years later. His name was Aldo Leopold and the book was called *A Sand County Almanac*.

Born in Iowa in 1887, he came to Arizona in 1909, fresh out of Yale with a degree in forestry. In 1916, he was at Soldier's Camp giving a lantern slide show on game preservation to forty residents. He told the audience that he feared the finishing of the new road on the north side (the Control road, the dirt route completed in 1920 that was one way in the final stretch near the top and entailed waits of an hour or two) would threaten the wild animals of the mountain because it would make the place easier for human beings to reach.

He was on the mountain to make a game survey which, like so many projects in Leopold's life, was never really finished. The man was driven, charismatic, and quick to see the essential element in any heap of data. Lyle Sowls, now a professor of wildlife management at the University of Arizona, remembers as a student of Leopold's in the 1940s going hunting with the old man. He would be driving along and get so wound up in his thoughts and words that Sowls would have to gently remind him to shift out of second gear.

Sowls met him by accident. Fired from his job tending cows at the University of Wisconsin dairy barn, he stumbled into Leopold's office as an unemployed sophomore seeking part-time work. The old man had recently injured his eye when a string broke on his hunting bow. Leopold made his own bows. He hired the young college student to read to him for hours each day, and Sowls discovered his life's work.

Leopold's study of the Catalinas found its way into a book (coauthored with J. Stokley Ligon and R. Fred Pettit but written by Leopold alone), and the book was never finished or published. It remains a draft entitled "Southwest Game Fields." The manuscript opens:

This book is an attempt to write a new kind of natural history. The early naturalists regarded a species as merely one of the phenomena of nature which needed to be discovered, catalogued and described. . . . "Gentlemen, look at this wonder," they said, and then set about to catalogue it, comfortably assuming that only the same blind forces which had caused it to be could, in the fullness of time, cause it to perish from the earth. But it soon became evident even to cataloguers that this comfortable assumption did not fit the facts. . . . On the contrary, the very civilization which at one moment held up a species saying, "Gentlemen, look at this wonder," might next throw it down and destroy it with all the nonchalance of a glacial epoch.

Leopold had no doubt about what his countrymen might toss away. The second chapter of this manuscript is entitled: THE VIRGIN SOUTHWEST AND WHAT THE WHITE MAN HAS DONE TO IT. He patiently ticks off the cost of overgrazing, overtimbering, the loss of the grasslands, and the surge of brush across the hills. He finally reaches into the Old Testament and offers up Ezekiel's protest: "Seemeth it a small thing unto you to have fed upon good pasture, but ye tread down with your feet the residue of your pasture? And to have drunk of the clear waters, but ye must foul the residue with your feet?"

Writing in the 1920s, he stares ahead to the Sunbelt:

This very diversity of climate and water supply which made these hills and plains a treasure house of wealth and beauty likewise made them a fragile dwelling for the modern white man. The engines wherewith he conquers these rocks and rills and templed hills are stronger than his understanding of what hills are, and more powerful than his vaunted love for them.

The book plunders historical records, ranges through game statistics from California, New Mexico, Indiana, and Pennsylvania—a sea of numbers, questions, and theories. It eventually collapses in a thicket of management tactics and guesses. Somewhere buried within this compendium of reports is Leopold's work in the Catalinas and like that game survey, the book itself can find no real ending or conclusion.

What Leopold glimpsed in the Catalinas, and on the other mountains he roamed in the teens and twenties of this century, comes across most clearly in his stabs at a preface to the book. The thing is typed, then penciled, and then has more penciled pages flapping along behind it like pennants. He is clearly gnawing on an idea that is hard to get just right but something that cannot be satisfied by tables of deer-kill statistics and chapters on manipulating species populations for the sportsman.

He scribbles in pencil, "It is perforce a hybrid sort of book." But he does work up to one announcement at the end of his first few pages:

Our attitude toward wild life reverses the usual assumption that wild life should be conserved in so far as compatible with economic development. Our conviction is that economic development should proceed only so far as is compatible with the conservation of wild life.

As he sadly notes, "Even among those who were born in the Southwest, not one in a thousand realizes what has happened to it,—that much of the beauty is the beauty not of life, but of dissolution."

Leopold concluded that in the Catalinas the coming of the white man meant the wolves, bighorns, bears, antelope, and wild turkey had declined or disappeared. He himself was part of this extermination in the Southwest. One famous essay he wrote late in life recounts shooting a wolf in northern Arizona: "We reached the old wolf in time to watch a fierce green fire dying in her eyes. . . . I was young then, and full of trigger itch; I thought that fewer wolves meant more deer. . . . But after seeing the green fire die, I sensed that neither the wolf or the mountain agreed with such a view. . . .

"I now suspect that just as a deer herd lives in mortal fear of its wolves, so does a mountain live in mortal fear of its deer. . . .

"In wildness is the salvation of the world."

Leopold's posthumous book slowly gathered a following and went on to become a classic and like most classics was more read than understood. Where Leopold pleaded for wild ground, the book became a bible for people who thought natural beauty should be preserved, not natural systems.

A Sand County Almanac ends with a warning that perhaps began growing in Leopold's mind when he gave that 1916 slide show at Soldier's Camp and feared the coming of the new dirt road:

The trophy-recreationist has peculiarities that contribute in subtle ways to his own undoing. To enjoy he must possess, invade, appropriate. Hence, the wilderness that he cannot personally see has no value to him. Hence the universal assumption that an unused hinterland is rendering no service to society. . . . Do I need a road to show me the arctic prairies, the goose pastures of the Yukon, the Kodiak bear, the sheep meadows behind McKinley? . . .

Recreational development is a job not of building roads into lovely country, but of building into the still unlovely human mind.

The scrapbooks must weigh fifty pounds and they are merely fragments of her mountain. Gerry came up as a high school girl on the back road and stayed at a Summerhaven cabin. Now she is older and so is Summerhaven and as she sits in her Tucson kitchen and thinks back on that time in 1945, it is like reconstructing a lost planet.

The Summerhaven she discovered in the middle forties was a small alpine village populated by cowboys. On Saturday night in the years just after the Second World War, there would be a Western band on Saturday night and a dance. Men would fight and everybody would get a little drunk.

She knew Buster Bailey back then, bought a mare from him. The young woman found Buster, then approaching his forties, to be crusty, gnarled, in love with his horses—all mares—and a loner. Now she is middle-aged but her brown eyes sparkle and her voice frolics with a kind of music.

When John Brinkley was twenty-seven, he met her on the mountain and in 1948, they married. He was a forest ranger who had come to the Catalinas in 1945 and started with the Forest Service by packing supplies between Palisades and Lemmon Rock and later worked on a lookout. The young couple set up housekeeping at the Palisades Ranger Station, then an outpost with cabins, corrals, and as yet no road down the front side to Tucson. They cooked on a wood stove, read by a Coleman lantern, and for seven years, 1950–57, Palisades was their home, a place on the crest of the range surrounded by ponderosa. Until the early fifties, only about three families wintered over in Summerhaven.

There would be twenty or thirty Merriam's turkeys about the place—the descendants of a restocking in the 1940s. Abert squirrels (introduced in the forties) moved through the trees, and once, climbing down the ladder from the fire lookout on nearby Mount Bigelow, Gerry came face to face with a black bear.

John Brinkley came from North Carolina and had joined the Forest Service as a lookout on Mount Mitchell back home. John showed her his Catalinas, and she smiles, "Of course I just fell in love with the outdoors and the adventure."

He was an intense man and did not do things by half measure. The Catalinas became his mountain, and he gave his life to the range. In 1952, he tried the Sangre de Cristo Mountains in northern New Mexico. Gerry liked the change. There was more wildlife and she finally saw an elk. John did not want to stay.

"He loved them," Gerry explains in trying to express his feelings for the Catalinas. "They were his whole life. He wanted to be there." So they came back.

"It was the knowing," she continues. "He knew every canyon, every rock. The challenge, too. The Catalinas are rough. They're kind of a rockpile."

When people got lost in the Catalinas, John Brinkley would direct the searchers. He'd say just head down this canyon until you get to this rock and so forth and you'll find them. He was written up in the local newspapers from time to time as the ranger with a sixth sense. Sometimes the search-and-rescue team would just be outfitting up in Tucson and word would come that John Brinkley had found the lost person. It was the knowing.

His favorite country was Montrose and Romero canyons on the north side, the cuts in the mountain which wound down to Buster Bailey's old ranch.

Up on top, he fought fires, directed the crews, rode horseback through the range, and just lived out-of-doors. He and his wife would saddle up and be gone for a day or a week. He was about five feet eight inches tall and solid.

"He was one of the old-timers who set the standards," Gerry offers. "No swearing around women. No drinking."

But there was that intensity. At times he drank and drank hard, and then one August 18 he stopped, just like that.

Gerry remembers the road being finished on the front side. She took her first solo drive in her life up the new highway. She thought the new road was wonderful. It made the mountain so much closer to the city, so much easier to get into.

Then things began to change, little by little. More people came up the new road, more drunks. There were more car wrecks, more traffic, and more trash. They never used to lock their doors, and then one day they began locking them. People would come to the station—hurt from falling off rocks—or they would run out of gas or crash off the highway. John Brinkley spent part of his time scraping them off the pavement.

It was not something that happened instantly but was more a gradual kind of change. Take skiing on the mountain. In 1948, a quarter-mile run existed at Bear Wallow, Lowell Thomas, Sr., zipped down the short course of powder and said it was wonderful to have a ski area out in the middle of a desert. John and Gerry liked to ski Bear Wallow and when Thomas's remark prompted the Forest Service to begin planning a ski run and lodge on Mount Lemmon, it sounded fine to them.

But when the thing got built it was not so fine, a bulldozed implant slammed onto one of the mountain's quiet slopes. And then the radar station came, and observatories on Mount Bigelow, and a forest of radio towers and new picnic areas and more recreation areas.

Until the new highway, the mountain was almost innocent of picnic tables. In 1918, the Forest Service budgeted $100 to pack in supplies to Bear Wallow for three picnic tables, one fireplace, one toilet and two register boxes, a hitch rail, and spring development. Nothing came of this proposal.

Between 1922 and 1924, some facilities were finally put in at Soldier's Camp (a rest area for soldiers fighting the Apaches in the 1870s and 1880s), a first for the mountain.

During the 1930s, the Civilian Conservation Corp ran wild in Sabino Canyon. One hundred eighty men built the road and the stone bridges. They also put in wooden picnic tables, all burned for firewood within three months and replaced with concrete ones. By 1940, the canyon had restrooms, garbage cans, swings, and 100,000 visitors a year. A dam and an acre-and-a-half lake were created in lower Sabino and fishermen packed the place. The lake soon filled with silt. The lake was dredged in 1950 and silted in again within six months.

Up on top, nothing really happened until the highway hit in 1950. The CCC had fiddled around Bear Wallow in the 1930s, but real efforts to put in picnic areas began in the late 1940s as the highway neared completion. Molino Basin got thirty tables in the winter of 1947—48 (with fifteen more planned), and Bear Canyon got thirty-eight. The high country had one body of water, Soldier's Lake, a rock and masonry dam finished in 1923 and sponsored by local cabin owners. As early as 1933, Rose Canyon was eyed by Ranger Gilbert Sykes for a possible dam and lake and talk got serious in 1954. The lake became a reality in 1960.

"Everything began . . . ," Gerry tries to explain. "What shall I say? The use of the mountain began starting in our eyes to mushroom."

Firefighting changed also. Where before it had been John Brinkley and his twelve men, now firefighting became a kind of modern warfare with aircraft, SWAT teams of smoke jumpers, a huge coordinated campaign directed by people off the mountain, and keyed around bases of men and air fields. The fun kind of went out of the thing for a man like John Brinkley.

Fire for Brinkley was a passion, a violent threat, in his eyes, to the mountains he loved. And so fighting it personally meant a lot.

He was not a walker of the mountains. The man would not move one boot in front of the other if he could get hold of a horse. For years he favored a mule named Bea, and by the late 1960s rode a horse called Lucky, seventeen hands high and 1500 pounds. He rode horses everywhere, on trails and off trails. By the early 1970s something seemed to catch up with him. He had asthma and the attacks grew worse. He was a man who had always gone through periods of depression.

"He wasn't happy with the changes," Gerry says, "especially if they were changes that weren't going to add anything. The impact of people—more use, more people, more tramping around."

The man who loved the mountain planned a trip into Romero Canyon with his wife, into his favorite part of the mountain. And then before the trip took place he took his own life.

Now that is years past, and there is constant laughter in her speech. She has this pile of scrapbooks, huge scrapbooks with newspaper articles, photographs, and clippings on the mountain going from the early 1950s forward.

The clippings are lost men, lost children, crashed airplanes, fires, fires, and more fires. One yellowed story from 1956 has a photograph of Buster Bailey, boots off and hat pulled down over his eyes, taking a break from fighting a big blaze in upper Pima Canyon.

There are editorials asking for new roads so more of the mountain can be opened to automobiles, asking for peaks so scientists can build more observatories, and questioning wilderness areas as selfish and backpackers as a tiresome minority. The history of the mountain and the forest flickers across the yellowed clippings as arguments, scorched trees, injured people, and car wrecks.

In the old books the mountain hardly seems to matter. The rock and bighorns and Douglas fir and oak and desert floor seem buried in talk of management plans and resource development. For Gerry surveying this past produces a curious sensation. In part, she relishes remembering the early days of her marriage on the mountain when the place was calm and isolated. And then she notes the various improvements, many of which she favored at the time. But finally, she faces a mountain that seems diminished from the one she first found. The great highway of 1950 has decades later become a different thing in her eyes. It is the people, she thinks. Projects and changes that seemed innocent when the city was small later seemed like grievous wounds when the city grew big. Now she lives in town and hikes the Catalinas when she can. The house is spotless and warm and bookcases hold a feast of texts on botany, birds, and similar titles. She is a vibrant woman who lives in the present and smiles at the future. But when she gives directions to her home, she says head toward the Rincons, then turn toward the Catalinas, then head toward the Rincons again and hang a left toward the Catalinas. She is off the mountain but she will never get away from the mountain.

He went up to hunt deer in 1937 and "saw the deer but never did get one." That's the way Tony Zimmerman, ninety-one, remembers his first visit to the mountain. Born in 1893, he had taught school in Arizona for decades when he made that trip.

"I was flabbergasted," the old man recalls. "I never got over it. I saw a sign at the store—LAND FOR SALE—and I began buying lots. I saw the future of Mount Lemmon as a Mecca for Tucson. And it's still in the making."

He is still a solid man, the handshake firm, the eyes bright and clear, the voice forceful. He reclines in a chair in his Tucson home by a wood fire dressed as a woodsman in green canvas pants, boots, and a red plaid shirt. He had to move off the mountain in 1982 because of his wife's ill health, but he still goes up there often.

"I got bit by Mount Lemmon," he smiles, "and I told the principal at the Tucson school where I was teaching one thing's got to give, either teaching or Mount Lemmon."

In 1943, he bought the store on Mount Lemmon and moved up for good. The place grabbed him by the throat. When he arrived, he thinks there were maybe twenty cabins on the mountain. Sometimes he would be up there all week and never see another soul. He loved the big trees of the high country, the giant fir and ponderosa, and he speaks with pride of one monster near his store that is seven feet in diameter.

"The pure air," he boasts. "I think a man will live ten years longer up there than down here. I was up there thirty-five years and never had colds."

After a while he built the Mount Lemmon Inn and opened a sawmill. "I always told my men never to cut a tree without a government stamp," he says. He knew John Brinkley and found him a good but difficult man, a man handy with fists and sometimes touchy about matters. But a man who knew the mountain.

Buster Bailey was employed for ten years by Zimmerman as a mechanic at the sawmill. He was honest, hard working, and Zimmerman remembers his horses, all females, and how he had them trained.

Zimmerman, Kansas born, was ripe for life in a mountain village. He had come to Arizona to teach school and in 1912 was teaching in the Blue River country over near the New Mexico border. The Blue was one of Arizona's last strongholds of the wolf and the grizzly, a place Aldo Leopold, then a forest ranger, knew as "the tangled canyons of Blue River, full of whitetails, wild turkeys and wilder cattle."

Fire near Summerhaven

One winter day, Zimmerman went hunting with a local man. They rode through in six inches of snow and Zimmerman dropped four deer with four shots. He was toughened by the land. In 1915, he taught school down on Eagle Creek north of the mining town of Clifton, and often on a Friday night he would take a lunch and walk the thirty-seven miles into the small community, returning on foot Sunday evening. That same year there was a teacher's meeting in the town and Zimmerman made a march of fifty miles in twenty-four hours. Ranchers along the way kept offering him horses but "I said no. I won't bother with a horse. I enjoyed walking."

During his teaching days on the Blue, he met Ben Lilly, a hunter who finally disappeared into legend. Lilly had started his search for lion and bear in the south and migrated across the southern arc of the nation pursuing his quarry. Once he guided Theodore Roosevelt. A religious man, he would pull his dogs off a hot scent on Saturday night and lie low over Sunday. Zimmerman recalls that if Lilly's long marches (he always hunted on foot in a loping gait) brought him within fifty miles of the school, he would stop by to give the children candy. When Zimmerman, the walking man, once went hunting with Lilly, he could hardly keep up. "Fifty miles a day was nothing for him."

Lilly traveled light, a half a dozen dogs, some corn meal for him and the animals. He bathed once a week, slept out year-round, and was soft spoken. In 1912, he took a huge grizzly out of Blue River, a reputed stock killer, and Zimmerman at ninety-one still remembers the hunt as an epic. He recalls Lilly setting out with seven dogs and four days later he was down to one little black bitch. He had gotten some shots into the bear, and he followed the wounded beast through snow up to his armpits. The hunter rounded a rock, his dog growled, and the bear came at the man. He fired and then pulled his dagger and stabbed the grizzly in the heart. The bear fell dead at his feet.

Lilly only carried a light blanket, and by now he was cold and half starved. He cut the bear open, and he and the dog gorged on raw meat. Then he retreated about fifty feet and built a fire under a big Douglas fir and broiled more meat. That night he threw his blanket over the dead coals and bunked until morning. He and the dog walked out ten miles at first light. That is the story Zimmerman recalls. As it happens, Lilly filed a government report on that particular bear and after he killed the grizzly, he struck the trail of a mountain lion. He instantly felt renewed and took off and killed the big cat also.

The bear itself, Zimmerman recalls, was eight feet around the waist and had an eighteen-inch paw. The last grizzly was slaughtered in Arizona in September 1935 and as the old man talks by the fire in his Tucson home, he is a link to an age in some ways as remote as the days of the megafauna when mammoths wandered southern Arizona.

When I was a kid I saw a painting in a book of Daniel Boone leading settlers through the Cumberland Gap. Behind the buckskin-clad frontiersman stretched a cavalcade of people and wagons, all the clatter and tools of that thing called civilization. Boone stares ahead at the endless virgin forest rolling ever westward. Zimmerman came to the Catalinas with some of that same mix—the man flabbergasted by the beauty of the place, the man who instantly starts buying land because he senses the potential for growth and development.

Not that he was greedy. When a fellow innkeeper on the mountain tried to talk him into raising his restaurant prices, he refused.

He told the man, "I like Mount Lemmon. I'm not here to make a pot of gold and get out. I'm here for good."

Come September the few cabin dwellers would pull out to put their kids in school and "there'd be nobody there." Zimmerman liked that.

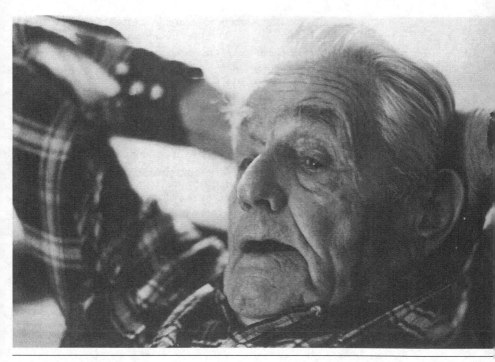

Tony Zimmerman

When the new paved highway was completed in 1950, "it went to developing and then came the Radar Station and that brought in plenty of workmen." And Zimmerman liked that also.

He was constantly on the alert for opportunities on the peak. When Randolph Jenks filed his mining claims in the forties and pried deeded land from the Forest Service, Zimmerman bought fifty-five acres from Jenks. When Jenks scouted around and tried to tie up the water rights to all springs in the area, Zimmerman created a water cooperative to shield his interests. He was instrumental in getting telephone service. "You can hear over those lines to London or anywhere in the world." As early as 1940, he applied to the Forest Service to put a ski lodge in where the present one now operates. He was too early, he says, and missed out.

The sawmill was his pride and joy and originally stood across from the store in Summerhaven. Finally, when the tourist trade built up, he moved the operation because he feared onlookers would get hurt. The new site was on Oracle Ridge near the crest, a spot he still holds as one of his favorites. From the high plot, he could see a hundred miles to Willcox and take in enormous sweeps of Arizona. In the forties, he peddled his lumber to Old Tucson, a movie set outside the city mocked up to look like a frontier town. From that connection, he made sales to Hollywood for yet more movie sets.

The movie people were quite taken with the view from the mill site and talked of building a sixty-room stone hotel, complete with narrow gauge railroad, ski lodge, tennis courts, and stables. The deal fell through when the moguls failed to buy out other interests on the mountain, a failure Zimmerman now allows may not have been a bad thing.

But whatever Zimmerman's second thoughts, he is firm in his faith in the mountain and its destiny as a developed resort. The man who walked and hunted on fifty-mile treks with Ben Lilly thinks a tramway would be a real asset for the peaks. As he speaks, his voice almost sings with the potential of the mountain.

"At one time," he brightens, "I knew the top of the mountain to be valuable. Every morning I'd take a shovel and a lunch and go up over the mountain looking for a place where I could find copper overlapping the top of the mountain so that I could file a claim on the top. I knew it would be a great place for airplanes to land."

The man who came here hunting the deer only killed one in thirty-five years of living on top. He was simply too busy with the store, the inn, the sawmill, the real estate developments, the plan for a ski lodge, the notion of a hotel, the prospecting for an airport site, and the raising of five children.

There are some regrets. Sabino Creek is now polluted from sewage overflows and that pains the old man. Some of the development has been ugly and brutal. He winces at the bulldozing done for the high-priced condominiums of the venture called The Retreat. But on balance, he looks back over the decades of change and smiles at what he sees.

He sits in his easy chair at ninety-one and I can practically feel the heat coming off him from the optimistic fires that rolled across this country in the great settling days of the nineteenth century. My doubts, hesitations, qualms, and the like are foreign to the old man. He loves the mountain and sees no conflict between what he has wrought and his love.

"I think," he says, "there's no limit to what we can expand to. There's lots of roads have to be built."

I am out of step with the basic drives of my nation, and Tony Zimmerman is those drives made flesh. He loves the forest and the sawmill, the pure air and the paved highway bringing long lines of cars spewing exhaust, and the quiet and the hundreds of new neighbors crowding into the few hundred acres of homesites. He sees and feels no contradiction.

I am drawn by the power of his drive. I ask the old man what he likes best about the mountain. He thinks and says, "I prefer the big trees, walking among the big trees."

This time the heart of gold is a restaurant planted on the edge of the slope above Cañada del Oro. Down below the canyon looks like a green mat of trees trailing off into the brown of the desert grassland. But here at 8,200 feet, the world is white with snow and the air raw as a wind whips through the January day. Skiers course down the runs in the bright sunlight of afternoon and many people rest and snack in the Iron Door Restaurant.

This time the story is a little different. According to a big sign in the entry painted in flowing script, Jesuits under Padre Kino ran the mine with Indian labor, chiefly Papago. After an Apache raid (the tribesmen according to the restaurant account attacked the place because in their simple state gold meant nothing to them), the mine was destroyed and the great treasure lost.

No one in the cafe seems too upset by the ancient deed. Wood burns in the huge stone fireplace and smiling women look up from the tables. They are young, the hair is blonde, the outfits bright with color, and the cheeks flushed from the mountain air.

The wind is a bit strong but all in all, it is a perfect day. I walk outside and glance at the forest of Douglas fir thriving below the summit on Lemmon's north slope. Fingers of white lace through the trees where skiers fly about. Two lifts haul them up the mountain to 9,100 feet, where the law of gravity graciously flings them back down.

The names of various runs compose a kind of poem about the mountain: Heidi's Meadow, Hot Dawg, Lemmon Drop, Gobbler, Crash & Burn, Aspen Ridge, Rick's Run, Becky's Way Out, and Jay's Chicken.

I have come to see one run in particular, George's Gorge, a slope for beginners in the sport. The snow is crusty as I start up an old nature trail, a short route once called Sabino Dawn, and powder bounces across the top like white sand. An Abert's squirrel watches me from a fir trunk and everything has the feel of a idyllic world of forest, snow, and alpine peace.

A sign stretched across the path warns:

DANGER

STAY BACK

THIS LINE

I go on. The nature trail abruptly ends and the forest goes away. Above me stretches a white channel for skiing. The area is mashed down now by the tread of a big snow cat, but soon it will be like the other runs, a white corridor of people leaning over their skis and flying down the mountain to feel the rush of speed and the smear of green conifers zipping past their gaze, the whole descent ending in smiles, laughter, and drinks at the Iron Door Restaurant.

This finger of snow where the forest once stood is the upper reach of Sabino Creek, the small stream that cuts the big canyon through the front range. The obliteration of the nature trail and the removal of the stand of Douglas fir was not a capricious act. Permits were applied for, the Forest Service reviewed and considered the matter, and everything was studied. Land of Many Uses.

Alongside the new run, huge logs are piled, big fir three or four feet in diameter. I place my hand against the rows of rings and my fingers cover a lifetime or two. This is the Canadian life zone of the mountain, a small dab of woods near the summit that mirrors in species and look the kind of forest one would find far to the north in Canada. Botanists have long marveled at the fact that such a stand of trees can be found on this towering island in the Sonoran Desert, just as skiers have marveled that their sport is possible sixty miles from the Mexican border. The snowfall in the Santa Catalinas is not dependable, and some years the skiing is more a hope than a

Felled Douglas fir

fact. But people are hungry for the sport, and with a growing city of half a million just below the peak, the place does not lack for customers today. Local T-shirts and bumper stickers advise, SKI THE LEMMON.

When the grove along Sabino Creek was cut for the new ski run, people discovered something they had not known. They found out a little about the trees they killed.

One, now a stump near the top of the run, had lived quite a life as it turned out. The rings on the flat stump revealed the fir had been growing on the slope since 1430.

It had been, at least until October 1984, the oldest known living thing in southern Arizona. Nobody has much of a handle on what time means to a tree. But we can make stabs at what time means to us: when Columbus set sail to discover a new world, the fir was 62 years old; when Cortez burned his fleet on the beach and marched to the Aztec capitol, it was 89; when Thomas Jefferson penned the Declaration of Independence, 346; and when Tucson became an American town on the desert below, 423.

Aldo Leopold warned about the danger of the road when the big fir was 486. Tony Zimmerman came hunting his deer during year 507. John Brinkley first worked the mountain that became his life when the tree hit 515. And when I first glimpsed the range, the big conifer was 527 years old. At the age of 554, the clock stopped for the fir and time caught up with it.

The day is absolutely perfect except for that wind. The sun flashes off the snow and powder dances along sparkling in the light. The skiers, the gaily dressed skiers, fly down the slopes and beam when they make the run and laugh when they fall.

I sit on the pile of huge Douglas fir logs and watch people enjoy the mountain.

The southernmost ski area on the North American Continent. You can be swimming, golfing, playing tennis or working in the morning and still run up at lunch time for an afternoon on the slopes. . . .

The slopes are groomed and waiting. . . .

Mt. Lemmon Ski Valley is located in the Coronado National Forest and is working with the Forest Service to continually improve its skiing facilities for the benefit of the many skiers who have taken up the challenge. We extend the same challenge to you. Can you handle it?

We're waiting.

Brochure, Mount Lemmon Ski Valley, 1983/84

THE FRONT

No man or beast ever scaled the southwestern wall of the
Santa Catalinas.

"RAMBLES AT RANDOM THROUGH AN ATTRACTIVE
MINERAL AND PASTORIAL REGION,"
ARIZONA WEEKLY STAR, AUGUST 18, 1881

During the six days from April 7 to 12, 1902, [we] made
an interesting trip into the Santa Catalina mountains. . . .
The region is rocky and inaccessible by wagon, conse-
quently we were forced to go on foot and pack our camp
equipment on burros, after reducing it to a minimum . . .
The burros were poor and unfit for use. . . . One was abandoned on the last day and left among the rocks to recuper-
ate as best it could.

ROYAL S. KELLOGG, "REPORT OF A TRIP INTO THE
SANTA CATALINA MOUNTAINS,"
FOREST SERVICE REPORT, APRIL 1902

Wild blooming prickly pear, wild cottontail, wild tee shots.
Here at Ventana Canyon, nature's as much a part of your
day as a round of golf . . . First, a scenic championship
golf course, designed around natural rock formations at
the base of the spectacular Santa Catalina Mountains . . .
A superb dining area and bar lounge looking out to the
mountains. . . .

"EXCLUSIVE BY NATURE" ADVERTISEMENT, *VENTANA*
CANYON: THE COUNTRY CLUB COMMUNITY, 1984

Everyone apparently favors having a reserve and realizes
the good it would do. . . . There are no mining claims in the
limits of the proposed reserve, and no other complications
to make trouble as far as I know.

ROYAL S. KELLOGG, FOREST SERVICE REPORT ON
SANTA CATALINAS, 1902

The satellites coursed by in squads and the wind kept the city
sounds away. We lay on the rock sheet at 7,000 feet and stared at
Mount Kimball, Window Peak, Cathedral, Mount Lemmon. The
mid-March night fell like a stone, heat ebbed from our perch atop
the high cliffs, and then the cold hours came. We heard nothing but
wind and saw nothing except the stars. Then, after midnight, the
constellations vanished as clouds rolled in low and angry.

First came the light rain, then stabs of ice, and finally around 3
a.m., snow. The winds gusted up to fifty miles per hour and ate deep
into our light down bags sheathed in nylon cocoons, things called
bivy sacks. We awoke to a world gray and white, to water frozen in
the canteens, and snow filling the coffee pot.

This is the front range, a wall of stone that looks pasted against the sky like a decal. The trails are steep, the water scarce, and the mountains display bare bones of rock. For most people the front range is the Catalinas, the skyline they see each day, the canyons they day hike now and again.

People sometimes ask me if you can be alone in the Catalinas, if there is a shred of solitude left in this rockpile next to a city of booming past 500,000 to a million or more. Yes. When I hike the high country, except for a few easy loop trails near the parking lots, I seem to see no one. When I camp, I never know what weather the range may deliver up in my sleep. The trails sometimes seem like stone ladders up cliffs and the climbs make the Grand Canyon seem not so bad when you hit its fabled trails.

At 3 a.m. when the snow finally comes, I roll deeper into my bag and harangue myself for once again going to the mountain in running shorts and a T-shirt, for once again dismissing them as a kind of city park.

We entered on a sunny day that offered the promise of summer. We moved through saguaro and agave under a hot sky and the water fled our bodies. By the time we hit the oaks and a stream at 6,000 feet we were down three quarts apiece and wondering about the available supply up ahead. We hiked slowly up to a saddle under Mount Kimball and suddenly another hiker came charging down the trail, face red from the sun, and his eyes asking for water, water. He said he had a gallon in his pack but wondered if that was enough and headed down past us to the stream.

All the way up, we have the city at our backs, a living, crawling thing probing the desert with subdivisions, roads, and machines. The canyons of the front range all stare down rock slots at this target and yet the big mountain does nothing as the city comes nearer, as the noise grows louder, and as the roads and houses hack at the slopes and stab into the ancient calm.

Townhomes against Pusch Ridge

In 1978, almost 57,000 acres of the front range were locked up as an official wilderness, a place free from roads and machines. The newspapers at the time were full of arguments about whether a place this close to the clatter of the city could ever be legitimate wild ground. When I sit in town, the notion of an officially designated wilderness area in such a place seems like a joke. When I lay in my bag on a rock shelf near the lip of a cliff while the wind races and the snow stings my face, I'm not so sure. I am seven miles from the truck and much less as the crow flies. I can stand and stare off the cliffs at the city below, an electrical firestorm organized into squares and bleeding energy into the sky.

I reach out of the bag and search my backpack for the food bag. I grab a granola bar, rip off the foil wrapper, and bolt down the conglomeration of nuts, seeds, chocolate, and marshmallows. Then slowly but surely comes the warmth, calorie by calorie stoking the billions of furnaces in my body. The grip of the night storm retreats, the small nylon bag seems a safe world, and the mountain, no longer a menace, becomes a living body of stone, plants, and animals that tolerates my presence.

I walked in twelve hours before as a circuit flashing phone messages, bills, things to do, and things that will never be done. My body lurched and fumbled, a ruins, and the first few miles the mountain functioned as gymnasium where I pounded out my tensions. I stopped and doctored my feet. I stopped and devoured a sandwich. I stopped and stared at a swift careening off a canyon wall and watched wind work the brown grass on the hillsides.

This thing celebrated as Nature in all the books did not exist for me. Instead, I marched through a clutter of rock and plant and weather.

The storm, something about the storm, fixed that emptiness and all the other matters. There was the granola bar, frozen like a rock, melting in my mouth. My hand reaches from the bag and the ice stings, the fingers go numb, and the air licks across the flesh.

The mountain and I lose that distance and I am locked into the pulse of the thing. I shiver, watch, and wait. I am no longer a visitor.

The word "wilderness" puzzles me. Wilderness should mean Daniel Boone, big game, landscapes empty of straight roads and powerlines. The buffalo graze, the Sharps rifle cracks, and raw, hot liver smears against my lips. Five days across an empty plain and not a single footprint. Things like that.

But here I am and this is an official wilderness and I'm seven miles from a boomtown, a fancy hotel, a bar with wine served in delicate crystal. And yet I agree with that designation. I want to believe in that reality and now with the cold and the snow on the cliff, I do believe. It has taken me years to get to this place and this sense of things.

I am the product of childhood glimpses of images in books, of tiny scraps of experience gleaned from the noise of a century hell-bent on industrial growth.

The car stops by the two-lane road. The morning air hangs with mist and it is 1954 in Yellowstone park. I am nine years old. I get out and stare. Coarse grass glows electric green in the dawn light and then the bog begins, a slate of gray water steaming beside the safe pavement. The moose does not lift its head and continues to feed. My father smokes a hand-rolled cigarette and stands there in a T-shirt, trousers, suspenders, and polished leather shoes. My sister aims her Kodak hopefully into the murk. Other cars stop and people get out and look and say moose and look again. Yellowstone park delivers on all its promises.

In a week, I am back in a Chicago apartment, people walking over my head, the streets never silent. The moose lives on in my brain.

That is the American wilderness, a set of primal images hammered out by romantics like John James Audubon in the nineteenth century, cast into words by Emerson, Thoreau, and all their descendants, and served up on slick paper in the dying days of the twentieth century as huge color plates in calendars, thick slabs of paper called coffee table books. This wilderness is always a reservoir of what we profess matters to us as a people, a sacred turf where we imagine the possibility of renewal regardless of our sins and all those empty bottles of Jim Beam scattered about the living room floor. This wilderness is always safe, a place where the mosquitoes vanish from the camera eye, the sunsets flare red, the wind is gentle, and the grizzly bear, the big bear that eats us, is not a foe but an endangered species, a thing we must care for and nurture lest the sacred spot disappear and the pulse of energy we feed off suddenly fall still.

We almost never go to this American wilderness and when we do, the visit is brief and usually from a car window or safe in the glow of a fire burning hot in the main hall of the lodge. We are reluctant to walk this place and many of us spend our lives far from its locale. But we believe in it just as surely as we believe in personal computers, cable television, and the necessity of progress. And this makes us a peculiar people.

This wilderness is a fantasy and a fraud but knowing this spares me none of its power. I am the child of this place that does not exist.

I hunt for reports of this powerful country and they never come when I expect them or from sources I anticipate. Sometimes the snow arrives at 3 a.m. and slaps awake with the sensations of worlds I cannot control, and I feast.

Sometimes the wilderness is a mountain, a big mountain topped with fir and pine and called the Santa Catalinas. And sometimes it is flat, hot, and covered with cactus and creosote. No matter. I know the place and it is always the same.

Once I stumbled on the place and the place was a man. I met him by accident but that is usually the way. When he was a boy, his mother told him, "As far as the tribe and the family here, you will always be on the outside. You started out on a different road."

When he was a boy, he watched his great grandfather catch rattlesnakes for the deer dance. The old man used his bare hands, and he told the boy he would never be quick enough to catch rattlesnakes himself.

Now the boy is an old man and he sits in a job training office on a Papago reservation in southern Arizona, chainsmoking, drinking coffee, and barking orders. I am here because a young Papago, a man of twenty or so who had quite a reputation as a baseball player, wandered away from his home one day. They found him hanging from a mesquite tree. The old man had taught the young man in the job training program.

The old man is named Eleasar Celeya and he does not want to talk about the suicide in the desert. It will do no good, he explains, and I let the matter go.

The office hums with energy as Celeya lashes young Indians toward lives as electricians, his own trade. He calls them blanket asses, waves his hands, examines blueprints, and answers a phone that never stops ringing. His students are drunks, misfits, people who by their twenties wear the brand of defeat. All this is foreign to Celeya.

But then he comes from a different world. The Papago were once the desert people, human beings who could live and thrive by farming, hunting, and seed gathering within the scant rainfall of the Sonoran Desert. And among the Papago was a subgroup called the Sand Papago, who lived a life of total wandering in the fierce desert of western Arizona and northwestern Sonora. In the 1850s, an epidemic wiped out most of the Sand Papago and in the 1890s a posse of Mexicans slaughtered most of the survivors, a small group of Indians who frightened Americans, Mexicans, and Papagos alike with their zest for banditry and murder.

Eleasar Celeya is a Sand Papago, a kind of living fossil who sits in an office scanning blueprints with a cigarette constantly dangling from his lip. During the Second World War, he went into the Army, became a ranger, and survived twenty-eight island landings.

After the war, Celeya went into the trades and became a foreman on electrical crews, and now, decades later, he has returned to the reservation to try and teach the young how to survive in a world that pays little heed to the old lessons of the Sonoran Desert.

But that is not what we talk about. There is a past, a time when Celeya was a boy that draws me. He never flipped open a book in a branch library on 79th Street and saw a line drawing of a moose feeding in a bog. He offers no memories of big game posing by the road in Yellowstone National Park. He was raised inside the wild country that I can only know in fantasy.

His great grandfather made his bows from cat's-claw and aged the wood six years. The shafts of the arrows came from arrowweed and for tips, the old man favored the springs off a Model T Ford, leaf-shaped for easy removal. Celeya's mother and grandmother were "Earth Magicians," healers. But the great grandfather taught the boy and made him a proper man.

He was told to run like a wolf, head swaying from side to side taking in the country. Sometimes, he and the old man would run all day. He learned old prayers, the correct way to breathe, how to find water, how to take game, how to kill with a knife, and how to flourish in a desert of three to seven inches of rainfall a year. When the two hunted, the old man would range ahead on foot locating the game. Celeya is still convinced his great grandfather could talk to animals. He is shy on this point, offering book explanations like telepathy, but he believes.

When they camped at night, they would lie with a fire between them and just before the boy drifted into deep sleep he would hear the old man's voice droning, a voice slipping into his mind and telling him how to live, something Celeya still calls simply, The Way. The boy could not recall learning how to hunt, how to read sign, how to notice the wind, observe the actions of the birds, and sense the movement of life across the land. All he remembers is that droning voice coming across the fire and then this sense of knowing.

The old man would dispatch him alone into the desert for two or three days at a time with a gun, a knife, and some salt. He learned how to take the bighorn sheep, the antelope, deer, and javelina. He mastered the bow.

When the boy was twelve, his great grandfather put him on a horse with a .22 Stevens singleshot and sent him on a journey of a month's time. The old man told him in detail what each camp would be like, and the feel of the land flowed into the boy's head. When he returned, the old man grilled him. He wanted to know what the boy observed each day, what birds, flowers, plants, and tracks, which way the wind blew, and how the deer acted moving up the hillside.

The boy recounted everything he had seen, day by day. From time to time, the old man would interrupt and say no, no. You missed this or you missed that. The boy felt the old man had been along, that he had seen everything with him.

Eventually, the Bureau of Indian Affairs caught up with the boy, shanghaied him to Indian School, and after that his education was a matter of summer vacations when he would return to the village. At the school in California, the boy spent thousands of hours learning to be a farmer, draftsman, and electrician. He would write letters home and in one note bragged of beating a Hopi in a footrace of more than twenty miles.

When he came home that Fourth of July, his great grandfather met the bus in Gila Bend. The old man handed the boy moccasins and a straw hat. And then he took off running the forty-two miles home.

The boy followed the old man on a trail through the desert, but he could not keep up. From time to time, his great grandfather would veer off, picking and eating mesquite beans. But just when the boy thought he was closing the gap, the old man would disappear into the distance.

Celeya got home around noon after a five- or six-hour run. He plunged into the shade of a wet tarp strung in front of his mother's house. As he sprawled there, he felt his heart might explode. The old man was in the house washing up.

His mother asked, "How'd the boy do?"

The old man replied, "He's soft."

That was the end of the schooling. His great grandfather told the boy he would not see him again and went into the Pinacate country to die.

And now Celeya is an old man sitting at a desk with a ringing phone in a federal training program, idly telling me how he was trained up. He is fat and smokes too much and drinks coffee all day long, and he knows things I will never learn.

He would never lay on a rock at 3 a.m. with the storm lashing against him and feel a moment of discovery. He would know and the mountain would only confirm that knowing.

About 4 a.m. condensation starts to collect in the bottom of my sleeping bag and my feet get wet and heat flees my body. I peer out and see I am mired in a sheet of ice and slush. Snow caresses my face and the peaks stretch in the dim light beneath the energy of the clouds. I think of getting warm, of safe city streets and cozy beds, and I think of that old Indian who had once been a boy that had run through hot deserts, his head swaying like a wolf from side to side taking in everything.

I cannot take in everything because, because I have never been a user. A visitor, yes, a person of the book stuffed with the lore written by scientists and naturalists. A hiker, a hunter, an idle wanderer. But never a user. The users get to the heart of the matter, to the bloody mash pounding at the center of the thing we hide in our words like "nature," "environment," "wilderness," "ecosystem." I have walked hundreds of miles in the hot deserts and cold mountains and once in a while, I glimpse that better country where a human being and the ground fuse into one and operate on the same rhythm and feed off the same thing. I once walked forty or fifty miles of hot desert on a June night under a full moon, and I cannot remember the pain now or explain the things I do remember. But the moments of feeling home at last have been rare.

Eleasar Celeya was a user. If he taught me everything in his head, if he droned on while I have slept by the fire, he could not give me this knowledge. He himself can barely retain it, his office swirling with blueprints and that ringing phone. For him it is a memory, for me a world I only know by report.

A few hours before the storm struck high on the front range of the Catalinas, I sat in the late afternoon light and stared at two things: an old juniper and a rock. The tree was dead, the bark gone, and the wood silver with age. The big roots clutched a large rock, something wrested from the earth in the final moment of death when another storm had snapped the thread of life and lifted the big wood from the ground.

I toyed with the thing as an image, a frame of queer beauty, the angry angles of the roots, the suggestion of massive strength in the wood, the rock lofted toward the sky and held suspended until dry rot finally frees it to return to the earth. Nearby, a small stream streaked the rock, and ferns and moss glowed in the dark light. A hawk worried over my head, slowly gliding and tumbling, again and again, wondering over my lack of movement and my presence in such a place. All these bits and pieces were puzzles in some kind of aesthetic and I relished the view. But I was walled off.

When the storm hit, the wall fell. There was not a living thing in the range that was outside the pulses I was feeling, and for a few hours we were all one, riding out the explosion of cold, moisture, wind, and the fists of the weather hitting the old craggy face of the peaks.

That is the mountain of my dreams, the one worth saving, the one ignored in the Environmental Impact Statements, the master plans, the zoning hearings, the meetings, the loose talk of our efforts to preserve, conserve, and manage. That is the mountain that can be called alpine forest or creosote flat, the place that sometimes is within national park boundaries and sometimes is just there with no special tag announcing it on our maps.

We come to this mountain through our various filters and lives, sometimes as cowboys like Buster Bailey, or game experts like Aldo Leopold, as dreamers and plungers like Buffalo Bill or entrepreneurs like Tony Zimmerman. Sometimes as young brides like Gerry Brinkley or Forest Service rangers like John Brinkley. And we disguise this mountain with the language of our various occupations and preoccupations. But it is the essential thing, the core, that makes us lovers or makes us go away numb and mute about what we have seen and felt.

At 6:19 a.m., Jack and I get out of our bags because we can no longer stand lying still in the cold. Weak tea bubbles on the small stove and snow still swirls down from the sky. The peaks wear shrouds of mist and cloud and the sun forces through as a pale yellow disc. We pack up and head down a winding trail to the saddle and the cut into Ventana Canyon. In less than a mile we hit the fork to The Window, a hole in the rock fifteen feet high and twenty-five wide. This aperture can be seen clearly at times in the city below. In 1915 or 1916, a railroad engineer, M. M. McDole, decided he would go up the mountain to view the formation. He figured it would not take too long on a horse. The canyons boxed up and forced him into hard scrambles. By dark, he pitched camp in a little grassy area far below The Window. During the night his campfire spread and burned up his pants. He rode out that dawn in his underwear and never tried to see The Window again. The front range is like that—immediate, close, inviting. And then when entered: hard, slow, and hostile.

We slip down Ventana through a mixed forest of oak and pon-derosa. The stream forms deep pools and where the canyon walls pinch in, the water tumbles over falls. Snow blurs against the rock and the wind whips. Nobody is around.

According to the Forest Service's 1984 statistics this should not be so. The wilderness section of the front range, that slab roughly from Sabino Canyon west to the end of the range at the Sheraton El Conquistador Hotel, hosted 101,200 Recreational Visitor Days (RVDs), while the rest of the Catalinas' backcountry bustled with 505,000 RVDs. Sabino Canyon itself, what with its road and shuttle bus, had 237,800 RVDs (130,250 riding the tram).

Taken as a whole, the range had 1.3 million RVDs and this has been growing for almost a decade at six percent a year. By the numbers, the mountain would seem mobbed and in spots it is. In fact during the 1970s and early 1980s, automobiles were outlawed from Sabino Canyon itself in an effort to save the place from growing use.

Today, people sometimes wait more than an hour to ride the Sabino tram. The paved highway up Mount Lemmon chokes with traffic and during winter snows, the sheriff's department lets peo-ple up one at a time like a ration system.

David A. King, a professor at the School of Renewable Natural Resources at the University of Arizona in Tucson, has assembled these and other numbers in a paper called, "The Santa Catalina Mountains: An Exurban Forest." The mountain that peers from his pages is a kind of recreational machine ("Lift capacity is 400 skiers per hour. . . . Slope capacity is 700 skiers. . . . Only two of five years being good snow years. . . ."). Besides the onslaught of 1.3 million RVDs, 38,990 AUMs of cattle nibble the range. (An Animal Unit Month indicates the amount of forage required by a cow and her calf, a horse, or five sheep or goats). Seventy electronic sites stud the ridges booming police messages, radio shows, and television. Vandalism takes out a lot of signs and has led to the creation of a

Weekend at Summerhaven

cement creature called the Catalina Table for picnickers. King sees the mountain as a place with problems that present challenges.

I'm sure he is right. But sitting on a rock in Ventana Canyon during a snow flurry, I cannot fret too much about the local RVDs or AUMs or much else. I haven't got any numbers, but the view before me is clear and free of everything but mountain. The Catalinas left to their own devices have a great capacity for self-protection. They are hard, hard, hard. Spared roads, trams, ski lifts, hotels, cabins, and other cushions for intruders, they reduce everyone to their level, and this is a place where, at least so far, the damage declines, the vandals go back to Rome or somewhere and the snow falls like flowers on the cold rocks by the tumbling waters.

Two hours later, we are almost out and white primroses bloom by the trail on the saguaro-covered hills. A group of elderly day-hikers amble past on an outing from a retirement trailer park—grist for those RVD numbers. In twenty-four hours, we have fried our bodies climbing the slopes and been chilled to the bone by a snowstorm, and now we chat with folks in their seventies who have walked up the canyon a mile and see the mountain as a friendly city park.

I sit by a deep pool, and a game trail lances up the slopes. Up there, I see a cleft in the rock, a perfect lair I fancy for a lion. And I don't doubt a mountain lion uses the place. I am maybe a mile and a half from the Ventana Canyon Resort, a hotel flush against the range where suites can cost $880 a day. I look up and think lion.

A part of me goes through rituals of anger at the hotels and foot-hills homes peddling natural splendor as they destroy it with their presence and cement. And a part of me thinks of the lion padding about on the edge of this steak-and-lobster world.

After months of hobbling about the mountain watching a mine gouge here, a road cut there, a ski run topple an ancient fir, a cluster of cabins pollute a stream, I have softened my anger. I am begin-ning to believe the mountain might make it. If we pull back, if we retreat just a little, a freak may endure in our midst—wild ground a few hours from the car where you can get killed by the weather and feel weak as the waves of wild energy roll past.

It is days later now and I sit in the bar at the Ventana Canyon Resort. Out the two-story glass windows, the mountain melts away in twilight and a spotlighted waterfall bounces off a cliff. The waterfall is maintained by pumps, a bit of natural beauty built by engineers. The resort itself is that state called tasteful, the brick carefully selected to match the mountain, the grounds left as much as possible in natural vegetation. The saguaros lining the golf course are repaired with green paste when balls blast their skins. Mesquite trees have been moved and relocated in a pioneering effort to avoid the bulldozed look so common in the Southwest. Even a heart as cold as mine to development has to tip my hat a bit.

The cocktail waitress brings burgundy, room temperature, and a bowl of nuts. Everyone is dressed quite well, and the room holds the soft murmur of conversation. The carpet mimics a Navajo rug. The colors are all earth tones and pastels so soft the eye slides over them without pain.

My mind is a captive of experiences, and I drink to kill them. Five days ago, I walked off the mountain in long underwear and boots and stood in front of this hotel and hitched a ride into town. That night I went to the intensive care unit of a local hospital and for days watched a woman die, bleep by bleep as her body spiraled downward on the screens full of lines tracking heart beat, blood pressure, and respiration. The pulse would race up to 190, the blood pressure lingered in the seventies and then ebbed away slowly to the thirties and finally the twenties.

The room looked out on a patio where birds frolicked in the trees with spring lust, and the sun fell like a sheet of fire. The leaves throbbed with energy, the screens bleeped, and the green wavy lines converted life into form and number and vital signs. In the long nights, the place emptied except for the nurses, ourselves, and

Relocating mesquite and saguaros

Mexicans, a people too wise to think their sick can survive on modern medicine and machines alone.

Outside the hospital, the mountain towered and every few hours I would steal away and go out and look at it. The range seemed exactly like a flat cutout, a thing glued against the sky to the north. I would stare at the canyon and ridge where the storm caught us and feel nothing. The sight was too flat to be real. And then I would go back inside to watch the screens.

Now the dying is over, the body converted to ash, and the ash scattered on the mountain. I drink. The cocktail waitress is very polite, and no one mentions my three-day beard or shabby clothes, the work shirt, dirty trousers, or the purple jacket raked by thorns. The mountain has vanished from the window, and all that can be seen is a two-story reflection of the hotel bar painted against the glass by the lights.

The resort is a platform for seeing the mountain, one where the range is a vista out a saloon window, where the desert is scenery as the golf cart whizzes along, where the rock canyons are potential waterfall sites if a pump is cunningly engineered. There are greater menaces in life than this place and these things. I live in a world where you go straight from wilderness to dying rooms crackling with the sounds of high-tech machinery, and I should face up to this matter.

But it does not come easy. Some part of me sees the mountain as life, and the glass of burgundy in my hand, the machines tracking the heart and forcing the lungs to breathe, the golf carts and the soft, the civil conversation in the tasteful room sees all these things as less than life. When I was on the cliff shivering from the storm, I was a person. When I was in the intensive care unit, I was a thing. We all were things. To speak of these matters is instantly to drift into arguments about technology, the simple life, what is natural, and the like. And I am tired of such talk. I am the child of the greatest industrial explosion ever witnessed by the planet, and there is no forest I can ever disappear into. Wherever I go, I bring the world that created me lodged within my head.

I bury these thoughts, and order another drink. Six months ago, I was sitting in a chair in Cuernavaca, Mexico, reading a book of criticism by a Mexican intellectual, Octavio Paz. The page offered a pygmy funeral hymn as ammunition in some esoteric argument about modern aesthetics.

An animal is born, passes this way, dies,
And the great cold comes,
The great cold of night, blackness.
. . . .

A man is born, eats, sleeps,
And the great cold comes,
The great cold of night, blackness.

The sky bursts into flame, its eyes go out,
The morning star shines,
The cold below, the light above.

A man has passed this way, the prisoner is free,
The shadow has melted away.

The hymn rumbles through my head like a midnight freight. Here is what I have got: the memory of an old Indian who once ran like a wolf and read the wind like a book; a storm on the mountain that crushed me with its energy; a room of machines patiently tracking death; a poem by pygmies that means more than I understand. And of course, the glass of wine, the calm, tasteful room, and the resort peddling the Catalinas as vista.

I keep going back to the mountain, hacking my way through thickets of resorts, homes, and bundles of RVD statistics. There is something there that must be settled for me, and that I will probably never settle. I remember Eleasar Celeya telling me over coffee how his Sand Papago grandfather warned him he would never be quick enough to grab a rattlesnake with his bare hands.

I must work on my moves. I must get faster moves. I want to move past this Front, this taunting decal of a mountain glued up and flat and dull, go beyond this into a harder place. I want to grab with my bare hands.

FROG MOUNTAIN

Food she cooked for me;
I did not eat.
Water she poured for me;
I did not drink.
Then, thus to me she said:
"What, then, is it?
You did not eat the food which I have cooked,
The water which I fetched you did not drink."
Then, thus I said:
"It is a thing I feel."
I rose, and across the bare spaces did go walking.

S'HAMPATAKI NYIO'K [WISE TALK]
AT BEGINNING OF THE PAPAGO SALT PILGRIMAGE
IN RUTH UNDERHILL, *PAPAGO INDIAN RELIGION*

Deep down in his heart the spirit of the adventurer yet persisted. "We will all of us have made fortunes by then." That was it precisely.

"After us the deluge. . . ."

The spirit of the West, unwilling to occupy itself with details, refusing to wait, to be patient, to achieve by legitimate plodding; the miner's instinct of wealth acquired in a single night. . . .

To get all there was out of the land, to squeeze it dry, to exhaust it, seemed their policy. When at last the land, worn out, would refuse to yield, they would invest their money in something else; by then they would all have made their fortunes. They did not care. "After us the deluge."

FRANK NORRIS, *THE OCTOPUS*, 1901

Nothing much happens here. No trail cuts into this canyon on the northeast side of the Santa Catalinas, a vast tract commonly called the backside and running from the dirt road along Oracle Ridge on the west to the dirt road running through Redington Pass on the southeast. We have dropped a couple of thousand feet from the crest, a bushwhack with patches of snow, a deer flashing through the brown grass, clumps of spruce, pine, and fir, and now I sit on a rock by a stream crashing through a pile of boulders. The forest changes here from pine to oak; sycamores still bare of leaves in early April begin to claim the broadening bottomland that spills down into the desert below.

I can see no sign of human beings but my own boot prints. I can hear no engines, make out no roads, glimpse no aircraft, and find no well trodden pathway.

I haul out my map. As the crow flies, I am maybe a mile and a half from the paved Mount Lemmon highway, a half mile from the dirt back road up Oracle Ridge, perhaps ten miles from Tucson itself. The canyon looks ordinary, a steep roaring drainage crashing through rock walls and between towering trees.

I flip open Dave Brown's study, *Arizona's Tree Squirrels*, and read the beginning: "I once lived in California in the Santa Clara Valley—the birthplace of Jack London's dog Buck. The valley is now called Silicon Valley and is all electronic factories and residences, but that wasn't so in the 1950s."

A lot of American books these days begin with a sense of loss and I can understand why. I was born in 1945 and spent my first years in a stone house built during the Civil War. Before I could vote, a wrecking ball toppled the fourteen-room fortress to the ground and the ten-acre woods of hundred-year-old oaks across the lane gave way to a nest of fancy homes.

The canyon on the Catalinas' backside continues to hold glimpses of the promise that once graced the entire range. Below me, the bajada spreads bare of homes and resorts and as the foothills give way to flat desert, no subdivisions feast on the acres. With a few tricks of the eye—block out the monster smelter belching smoke just to the north at San Manuel, skip over the fence lines and ranch roads and mining scars on the hills—the place looks a little like it probably appeared four and a half centuries ago when Coronado stumbled up the valley below seeking seven cities of gold and a quick ticket to stardom.

For months I have asked others about this spot. Gerry Brinkley grew kind of misty eyed at the mention of the canyon and said, yes, yes, go there. Tony Zimmerman, the grand old man of the mountain, allowed that it was a fine place and confided he had some mineral claims lancing across the trees, rock, and swirling water.

One day I was in the tree-ring laboratory at the University of Arizona, the outfit that put together a pioneering time-table for the Southwest based on the whispered messages in ancient wood, and

I ran into Tom Harlan, a man who knows this mountain and many others. At the mention of the canyon, his eyes lit up and he pulled out a file full of photos taken in its upper reaches. A man stands under a big Douglas fir log jammed across the canyon walls like a straw. The big tree rests ten or fifteen feet above the man's head.

Harlan beamed and explained that in 1978 a huge flood roared down the canyon and ripped out everything in its path. Go there he said. By all means go there.

So we have come to this place. Jack is busy prowling the stream with his 4 x 5, tripod, and a fist full of frets about good light and bad light and all the light in between. We leave our packs under the trees as the sky begins to clot with thunderheads. It is sixty-seven degrees and spring is barely an idea here. No wildflowers bloom, the ferns remain a carpet of brown, and birds seem scant, the spring migration hardly begun. The trees offer no leaves, but here and there a branch swells with the growing energy of the buds.

Coming down the canyon, we wandered through a pile of feathers that had the look of a wild turkey. Further on waited a mound of fur covering several square feet, a pile innocent of any bones. And then the noise of rushing water and silence.

I decide to take a look around, but this goes against the grain. I am tired of walking. In the past few months, there have been hundreds of miles in the Santa Catalinas and kindred places across the Southwest, the boots slapping against the black volcanic rock of the Pinacate in northwest Sonora; scraping across the brown soil of the Cabeza Prieta creosote flats in a blind march toward the Colorado River; slicing down into the layers of rock in the Grand Canyon; sinking into the thigh-deep snow of the Kaibab Plateau in the white silence of winter; moving through the sparse plenty of the Mohave; walking along the Rio Sonoyta where peasants beckon from the huts and offer full mugs of tequila; skipping lightly across secret airfields favored by drug smugglers in the age-old traffic of the border; and always, always heading back and deeper into the mountain. The Catalinas have grown like a weed in my mind, and this rank growth has spread its roots and tendrils across the landscape of the Southwest.

Everywhere I go, I think I discover distant outposts and forgotten way stations of the mountain. For me the Catalinas have escaped the simple limits of geography and become an essence of wild ground.

Whenever I return to my city, the range snaps against the horizon and bristles with promise, a generous green mound beckoning me to come back and try my hand again. And so I am by this stream in this canyon and I am determined to stay put, to let the mountain rub against me, to stop my boots from trudging toward some biological Jerusalem I can neither describe nor doubt.

The stroll becomes a boulder hop across the leaping waters, and the oak and small thorny bushes lash my limbs and leave faint red lines where the spines and sharp branches slice my flesh. The sun feels warm and I take off my shirt. At my feet what looks to be a Mexican garter snake, a reptile grown rare, darts ahead seeking a frog to dine on. Twenty yards down the canyon, I find a frog dozing on a boulder, and I sit by it and share a little frog time.

A year ago, I visited some Papagos on the reservation west of Tucson and sat in a mud house drinking beer and wrestling with a trilingual conversation (English, Papago, and Spanish) that moved at the speed of a glacier. One old man ravaged by diabetes and booze refused to speak in any tongue but Papago, and through a translator he lumbered forth with this message for me: his people had another name for the mountain known to whites as Mt. Lemmon. They called it "Frog Mountain."

I asked him why and my query slowly freighted its way back into native words.

Because, he finally replied, that is what the old ones called it. The old man did not mention Navitcu, the spirit who dwells on Frog Mountain. He is said to be an evil one, although once he gave the desert people their first gourds, that essential utensil for dipping water. Navitcu carried the seeds in his heart. In the great gambling games, the women of the Papago and their language cousins, the Pimas, were willing to bet everything they owned but the gourd dippers. They feared angering the spirit.

After a great flood that, according to the Papagos, swept this region long before the arrival of our calendars, I'Itoi, the godlike Moses figure of the desert people, came upon Navitcu and the turtle.

I'Itoi said, "You have no right to be here. I have not created you." And he sent them south. Each night they made camp, the turtle taking an ear of corn from his heart, Navitcu a squash. Coyote trailed the pair and saw this and told I'Itoi. He invited them back. But it was too late. The two spirits were angry and said they would return only for the summers. The rest of the year the people could starve.

Sometimes Navitcu came at other seasons. The desert people felt his presence when their knees swelled or their eyes became inflamed. A cottonwood mask of the spirit survives, the eyebrows and chin-whiskers and a tuft on each cheek made from horsehair, designs scrolling across the face and the mouth displaying teeth that look ready to bite into the lives of those who fail to show respect. The Papagos and Pimas placated the spirit with ceremonies and ritual use of cornmeal, for Navitcu skulking on Frog Mountain made the plants grow and that act brought food into the people's lives.

One of the old songs was triggered by Navitcu and celebrates the giant saguaro:

The big mothers stand there.
The big mothers stand there.
Whitely, they flower.
Black dry.
Red they ripen.

Smelter, San Pedro Valley

We know what he looked like. He wore a kilt, the grim mask (or sometimes simply a sack thrown over his head), a topknot of turkey feathers, and usually came from the north making shrill cries no one could understand. Now he has been all but silenced. Perhaps he waits under the cliffs in the upper canyon for he is said to dwell under some precipice in the range. Like so many things on the mountain, he has been sapped of power by his brush with the might of our machine-driven world.

I look down at the frog frozen in the sun's warmth on the rock. Frog Mountain.

The canyon chokes on debris from the 1978 flood. I stand by a pile of boulders and logs eight feet high that the stream swerves to miss as it crashes through a stratum of black stone. Next comes a small waterfall, the channel wearing deep into the rock and pounding out bowl after bowl as the energy of the mountain forms a chain of plunge pools. Inches above the white foam some spiders have cast a large net, and I watch them feed on trapped insects.

The canyon keeps repeating these notes—small insects, water busy grinding out a path, piles of trees and big boulders tossed up like popcorn by the flood seven years ago. I clamber down a big jam and look back at huge logs caught between the crevices of a rock wall with the stream issuing from their midst like the plumbing of a city fountain.

At first the canyon strikes me as very ordinary, a place like so many in these mountains where everything is up and down and walls of rock and I dismiss the scene as commonplace. And then, as always happens, I sink into the feel of the ground and as the hours creep by, the canyon grows more special and finally becomes what the mountain's folds and slopes and cliffs and gouges always seem. Unique. The Catalinas offer no Yosemite Valley, no Mount Rainier, no sweep of alpine meadow, and they are easily discounted on the first encounter.

For a century, people have gazed at them and thought of other possibilities than Navitcu. Just to the east, a copper deposit waits under Marble Peale for global commodity prices to rise and propel it into a full-scale mining operation. Below me, cattle munch down the lower slopes and the desert. And everywhere around me, mineral claims lurk as sentinels of my culture's dream of the bonanza. I have a small pamphlet, perhaps seven inches by five, issued in 1883, and the yellowing document smacks with lust for this ground under my feet where today a Mexican garter snake opens the spring hunt with dreams of a frog.

"Prospectus of the Santa Catalina Stock Raising Co., Tucson, Arizona Territory," the cover announces and inside an offer as old as the American presence in this region shouts for attention. The second page boasts a map with concentric rings issuing from a proposed ranch headquarters to be built down below me on the flats by the San Pedro River. Where I now stand is on the edge of the nine-mile ring, and the whole design has the look of a military target.

"In presenting our friends with this little prospectus," the text begins, "it has not been our desire to offer anything new. We wish simply to give a few plain statements regarding the advantage this section possesses over any other for cattle raising."

Then comes the pitch. The winters are gentle, and the cost of keeping a herd in this country is light, very light. The cows will have calves, the calves will be branded and castrated and turned loose upon the land as steers, and then at three years of age, the steers will be rounded up and shipped to market. All this grazing and branding and rounding up will cost $2.50 per animal. And the market? The market is booming. Between 1872 and 1882, the West grew one hundred percent in population but the cows increased only thirty-three percent. The whole proposition is a natural.

Start with 2000 cows, sell only the increase as three-year-old steers, and the money over the course of ten years will roll in like

Cañada del Oro beneath Pusch Ridge

clock work. The first year, 1600 calves (800 heifers, 800 steers) will be born and the whole cost will be $2500. By the fourth year, the herd will number 10,200. Eight hundred steers will go to market and the cost will be $9000, the income from sales, $21,600. And that is only the beginning. In the tenth year, the herd will mushroom to 50,677 with 3,219 steers sold for $86,913. The cost will be $45,000 and the value of the whole operation will weigh in at $1,013,540. It will be 1893 and you will be rich, by God, rich.

This dream did not quite come true. The cows came and they did increase. But the land lashed back. In 1891, Arizona's governor estimated that 1,500,000 cattle were busy eating the territory. Then came drought and the cows dropped dead. Old reports claim that a man in southern Arizona could skip a stone across the region from carcass to carcass. The grasslands diminished or vanished, the streams and rivers fell away into the sands, and all the numbers proudly printed in pamphlets like that put out by the Santa Catalina Stock Raising Company, all these visions of big bucks went bust and ranchers went belly up.

The land I have come to love is in many ways a ruin left me by my ancestors, and as I stand in this lonely canyon on the Catalinas' backside I am viewing an invalid struggling to come back from a savage illness. I would not know this fact except for the books and pamphlets that track this orgy of greed and enterprise. I accept the landscape the way I see it and find it not wanting. But still, I must consider that it once was lusher, more diverse, and more teeming. Down below me on the flats, antelope once ran. Now they are gone. Above me on the peaks, bighorns once dominated, and now they are refugees on one isolated ridge of the range. The black bear clings in small numbers; the grizzly has not been seen for more than half a century. The jaguar no longer visits. No one hears the cry of a wolf.

So I come here from my city to relish a terrain that has been grievously wounded, a place that in some ways is a shadow of its former self. I can accept this fact. But what gnaws at me is the certainty that what I now find will be further diminished in the future. This fact does not go down so easily.

Behind me a side canyon knifes in. The gouge is almost barren, scoured down to bedrock and nothing but small saplings give a hint of green in this place. Water falls over sheer cliffs, and in tiny pockets I can find little piles of soil. But on the whole, this side canyon is a blasted place. The great flood of 1978 stripped it bare and now it begins the long march back to life.

I suspect the mountain can live with this kind of wound and has suffered such blows repeatedly since the range rose up from the plain. The surrounding slopes pump seed and animals into such a void, and the waters carry soil, and with time the wound will heal over and slip away even from memory. But the kind of assaults delivered by my kind, by human beings, are much larger, more widespread, and bite deeper into the fabric of life on the slopes. The mines do not nick; they rip. The cattle do not nibble; they devour. And unlike the flood, they can reach everywhere and do not visit just one rainy afternoon, but day after day, year after year. The roads come with fist of dynamite; the cabins spill new torrents of chemicals and sewage. The saws, if left unpoliced, cut until nothing but a sea of stumps remains.

For almost a century, Americans have grown slowly conscious of these facts and through a horde of agencies, through the Forest Service and the Park Service and the Bureau of Land Management, and through books of statutes outlining the need for clean air and clean water and enduring soil, trees, and wildlife, they have sought to heal and avoid the great blows delivered in the past. I stand at the tail end of these decades of conservation and I realize this effort has saved the ground I now walk on. But somehow these achievements are not enough to satisfy my needs.

The work of early conservationists, foresters, and range management specialists sought to ensure that the mountain could continue producing as an economic resource—keep offering up minerals and meat and board feet of lumber. I no longer share these goals. I do not care if the Santa Catalinas ever produce a single item that proves profitable to myself or my people. I want it left to seek out its own ends.

The day slips past and dusk comes to the canyon. The temperature begins diving toward the forties, and I sit in my bag under an open sky sipping a cup full of Canadian whiskey—100 proof just as Buster taught me. Stars come out and cold air flows down the drainage from the high country. The whiskey warms my throat, and hour by hour I watch the heavens drift across the bony fingers of the forest.

For generations, my people tried to scratch a living from American ground and most of the time they failed. They dug the ditches, drained the marshes, clear cut the forests, went down into the deep, dark holes and hacked the veins of ore, and battled as foot soldiers in the war industrial culture has fought with the virgin ground of North America. They stare at me wild-eyed and fierce in old photographs and I doubt they would understand my preference for a tree over a board.

I pour another cup of whiskey and the stuff flows down smooth, and each cup tastes better than the last. Ideas flicker across my mind like flavors teasing the tongue of a hungry man. There are now words for this need I sense in myself and books about the words. Conservation, environmentalism, and ecology have spawned a strange offspring called Deep Ecology, and philosophers argue within this new arena about a notion called a biocentric world, one based not on the demands of my species, *Homo sapiens*, but on the needs of all living things, even the pesky mosquitoes singing around my head as I drink.

I am not good at philosophy and have no appetite for chalkboards of equations. Abstract constructs tend to crumble in my hand, turn to dust, and blow away. I feed on experiences that are raw, rough-edged, and slow to digest. But I hear a kindred echo in this cumbersome word "biocentric" and accept the idea as something similar to what I feel, only all dressed up in Sunday-go-to-meeting clothes. I think much ground must be spared and left to forms of life as a place where they can fashion their own futures. And I think the Santa Catalinas are one such place among many. I have come to this conclusion through a set of experiences that seldom seem to bend to logic.

I down a pint of whiskey and listen to the mountain breathe night winds, and I feel the pull of the country. I came by my need for country honestly.

My father was called Jude and when he bought his wild 212 acres in Wisconsin and took me there, that was the ruination of me. He saw the place as a kind of crazy dream and made me a fellow dreamer. The memory is as fresh to me as the morning rain.

The rain trickled down the windows of our Chicago apartment as he sat there rolling smokes and explaining this new country. The property formed a horseshoe with the river forming the shoe. While traffic swished down the wet boulevard below, he talked of the swamp, which took up most of the land, and of the high ridge with pine, oak, and dry ground. The place touched no road, hosted no building. To his knowledge, no one had ever lived there.

The words tumbled out as he smoked: 212 acres on the Black River, downstream from the town of Black River Falls, county of Jackson, state of Wisconsin. Parts of the high ground had been nibbled at by lumberjacks but the swamp never was touched and he had paid five dollars an acre for land considered worthless. The river promised pike and muskie and bass but you had to walk dark timber through clouds of mosquitoes to reach this fishing. To enter his new acreage meant miles of dirt trail with the car groaning in the soft sand. The parcel touched yet more forest and bog and badlands, idle tracts empty of people and houses. A high line crossed the ridge but the property itself had no power, no well.

He sat there in Army fatigues, lots of pockets for all the things he liked to carry, and Army tennis shoes, the sides cut out with his pocketknife in order to air his feet. He wore a white T-shirt and baseball cap.

Ah, this is the place, Jude said between swallows of beer. Land free of a wall, a telephone, electricity. History bypassed this patch, floating high overhead like cirrus clouds on a cold day.

For weeks, he kept busy settling in: a thirty-eight-foot trailer dragged through the sand by a tractor. A generator from Sears, something he soon abandoned when he got an earful of the engine's noise. A Coleman lantern, a stove and refrigerator running off bottled gas, old dishes, and some books.

He hardly ever walked his woods. Jude sat and drank and read and fiddled with a little battery-powered radio for a bit of news. He never explained what he liked about the place and nobody ever asked him.

One day he suggested we take a hike. The start came in the early July dawn. Dew carpeted the grass and a mist breathed off the land. Jude polished off his black coffee and first smoke and then rolled a dozen for the trail, packing them in a worn leather case. No one else was up yet.

Shots of bird song fired from the trees and the growing sun drove the mosquitoes into the shade. We picked up our hats and nets and bottles of repellant and ambled down the ridge past clumps of beer cans the old man had hurled during his evening séances.

He cut a good stride, and the thinning gray hair on his head and the beer drinker's gut slopping over his belt did not seem to touch his legs. At times, bifocals gave a lurch to his gait but he carried his six decades of life easily. He was fifty the day I was born, and I grew up with a father who was an old man. He seemed at times like a creature from another epoch. He once told me sadly that I would never know all the names for the various and intricate harness parts required to control a working team. And then he rattled them off like some kind of song from a vanished tribe. But this distance of decades seldom registered with me. His arsenal of years held experiences that periodically surprised. Once he consented to help me with my fielding for an hour, and he batted the ball with ferocity and accuracy. Until that moment, I did not realize he knew what a bat was. When I was a teenager, he accompanied me to a pool hall to witness the prowess of my game, an activity which consumed me totally at the time. The old man broke and ran the table twice. We went home.

His early life had been hard manual labor, and the soft jobs in offices never seemed to touch this base of muscle and stamina.

I was twelve that July morning and my head was full of Little League. When Jude was eight, he drove a team in a sand pit and did a man's work. He and his brothers would sometimes touch fleetingly on early toils that rang like iron messages from some Dark Age of brute work. Sand pits, cutting blocks of ice in winter, ditch digging, corn husking, shocking, fencing, and traveling the farm counties painting barns and eating the slop of a hired hand. When he was twelve, he had hitched a ride hundreds of miles and rode a thoroughbred racehorse back to its new owner. I was twelve and had barely been downtown alone.

As we worked down the ridge into the forest, we were briefly children together. The trees cleared for an acre, and on the edge of a meadow a small pond whisped steam at the start of day. I always expected to see a deer in this kind of early light and never did.

Here the swamp began. The woods switched from conifers and oaks to strange, hard specimens, and the ground went soft. Saplings showed the gnaw of beavers and the mosquitoes worked three shifts a day. The air was insects and the clouds clogged your mouth and nostrils, covered your face, ankles, and hands. We put the nets over our heads and slathered chemicals on our flesh. From here on the cries of the swamp's hunger would never leave us for an instant.

The trail down the ridge surrendered at the edge of the muck and off to the northwest a hundred yards towered a cypress. At eye level, everything was a tangle of gooseberrys and kindred vines. As we crashed through the grip of the bramble, a rank odor like weeds floated around us. The big tree marked where the axes had stopped in the long-ago days of the great log runs. Small tracks of night killers patterned the ground at our feet, little marks of fox, mink, weasel, raccoon, skunk, and wildcat. Nobody went into the swamp much.

I followed the old man blindly into this green maze. He never announced a destination. Half water and half mud, the place lacked trails, landmarks, or physical definition. Each step forward brought a view just like the one left behind. As our feet sank into the mud, gases floated up rich with rot, and branches, tendrils, weaves, and nets of foliage grabbed our arms and legs, tugging, tripping, toppling us forward. The mosquitoes became a kind of white noise, and they busily probed our defenses and found gaps between shirt and trouser, trouser and shoe. Dozens rode the nets just before our eyes. Overhead, the rising sun hunted through a canopy worthy of the Amazon. I thought, nobody belongs here, nobody, and my mind filled with movie horrors from the Congo.

Two to three hours into our expedition, we crossed our own tracks. Sweat soaked our clothes. We had come some kind of full circle.

The old man stands there in the weak light which filters through the trees and squints with his bifocals at the green wall surrounding us. I cannot tell if he is angry or happy. He takes a leak, squints again at the tangled growth, and curses. He is happy. Anyone could get lost in this goddamn swamp, he says. Look at the size of it, the tangle, the racket of life in all this muck and water.

We shuffle along, bugs crawling everywhere, his back covered with feeding mosquitoes reaching through the thin shirt. Swamps and such places swallow Daniel Boone dreams. The nature photographs of the deer framed by pine, of the fox hesitating on the fresh snow—these images are inhabitants of the glossy magazine page. The mosquitoes are here. Sweat streams across his bifocals and when he moves to wipe them the damn mosquito net gets in the way and he grunts. He pulls out a map he had sketched on another Zig-Zag wrapper and stares down at it a minute and then stares at the wall of green five feet away.

He harbored no romantic concept of the land. My father came from the generation that had been driven off the soil to the city, one of many waves rejected by the seeming bounty of North America and forced by poverty and landlessness to take industrial jobs. His people had failed in Britain, failed in southwestern Wisconsin, failed in Iowa, failed in Minnesota, and failed in Nebraska. And yet somehow after all this rejection, an appetite remained for the forest and swamp and hillside and stream. He did not speak of this and I never knew him to read a book or utter a thought about the matters now bundled up as conservation and ecology.

But standing there devoured by mosquitoes in my twelfth year, I knew the old man felt good and I felt bad. By noon, my will had long gone and the heat and insects terrorized me. My blistered feet sank into the ooze and my belly rumbled with emptiness. Jude kept crashing ahead, ignorant of direction, intent upon our destination. He seemed happy banging up against things and had little need of talk.

He used to tell me a story that I did not understand as a child. Mrs. O'Hara and Mrs. O'Houlihan were washing clothes at the village well when Mrs. O'Hara asked, "And who do the O'Houlihans spring from?"

"They spring from no one," the woman replied. "They spring at them."

I felt weak and powerless in the endless bog. He did not. The cities, yes, those cities where he had spent a lifetime wearing suits and ties, those places, I sensed, made him feel weak. But not this. He thrashed ahead of me working his muscle against the muck. He hated organizations, rules, and government agencies—an understandable hostility since he had spent decades working for the Internal Revenue Service. Things called modern conveniences were suspect. In automobiles, automatic transmissions were forbidden. Calculators were banned. Use a paper and pencil. Typewriters did not make one a writer. Pick up a pen. Air conditioning was unseemly and did not sneak up on him until he was in his seventies. Aluminum beer cans were simply a sin, as were electric knives, power toothbrushes, electric can openers, high-priced wine, fancy clothes, power brakes, power steering, power windows, vacuum cleaners with numerous attachments, and multi-door refrigerators. Maps, too, were dubious at best, and he and his sister tended just to strike out and cross the country innocent of such witchery.

We broke out in early afternoon. One moment we were pitching and stumbling through the green tangle and the next instant, the wall parted and we saw the river. A beach spread before us carpeted with small shells and the current ran silent and dark.

We sat on the sand safe from the mosquitoes and peeled off our nets and shirts. Jude lit a smoke and cleaned his glasses. He was very happy.

He said the swamp was a goddamn wilderness and there was no mystery, no mystery at all, in why in the heyday of the Wisconsin lumber industry, it had not been timbered off. Who the hell, he asked, would ever find their way in all that muck and mosquitoes? The swamp was good for nothing, something that could not be turned to account, something that went on its own way, you know?

An old fat man, he sat there on the warm sand with his smoke and told me how Daniel Boone had cleared out of Kentucky when he discovered a neighbor within eighty miles. Sucking deep on his cigarette, he offered that if Boone had found this swamp, well, he could have stopped moving. That's for damned sure.

When we got back, he had a beer and never talked about that day. He felt very good. There was nothing to say.

I have never really gotten out of that swamp. The years pile up and move past and I remain twelve, mosquitoes screaming around my head, the raw gases rising from the ooze at my feet. I am lost in a place I do not seem to want to leave. As I wander across decades, time passes yet remains still, a block of things swirling by my side, and I dive into this expanse of dawns and dusks and hot afternoons and long cool nights and sample small moments at my leisure.

Wherever I go, I stay in the swamp and that place has become a maze that crosses deserts and climbs mountains and paddles canoes down rivers safe from dams. I have never tasted a drug that approaches this tangle of land in power.

I do not speak much of these travels to others and I wonder if they explore the same country. For me, when I leave the cities, I go to a kind of magic mountain, and standing under the Douglas firs I can smell the deserts, and thirsting in the hot cactus flats of June, I hear the bite of the paddle on a swift river and round a bend where a deer stands drinking by the shore.

When I walked with the old man, I broke into a world I will never leave and that he never felt the need to explain to me.

Down in Sonora, Mexico, there is a red cone in the Pinacate country called Cerro Colorado. Some scholars think the cone was created by volcanic energy punching up through an ancient riverbed. The sides of the eroding hills have the look of alluvium, and around the base of the cone the old riverbed spreads out against the desert flats like a gray pudding. I think the Catalinas are like that red cone in the Pinacate.

For me the range cuts through a lot of strata in my life and spreads out at its base and touches other matters far distant from the simple confines of the peaks and slopes within the National Forest. The mountain begins in Arizona and reaches east to the Atlantic, north into Canada, west across the Mohave, and south deep into Mexico.

My plodding pace under a heavy pack somehow permits me to knife through time and distance. I have never been able to take time seriously, and I tend to skip the walls separating the past from the future and muddle around in a kind of endless present. Distance proves to be a barrier easily leaped over and left behind. On my mountain, the day expands and carries me to many faraway places. The digital watch flashing on my wrist tells me nothing of value as I move along.

I am walking under the pine and fir of the Catalinas and head down the drainage to the San Pedro River miles away and far below. Gray light of early dawn seeps over the Galiuros to the east, and a faint breeze worries through the trees. An hour later, my crampons grip the glacier hugging Orizaba in central Mexico and to the east the midmorning sun rides easily above the plate of clouds covering the state of Vera Cruz. I look up at the almost 19,000-foot white peak and my steps slice into the river of ice.

The coffee rolls bitter over my tongue and I enjoy a late morning break under the desert sun of western Arizona near the Colorado River. Beyond the small rock tanks of green water, the Lechuguilla Desert flows to the east. A golden eagle lands on a rock fifty feet away. We eye each other for minutes. I lie on the ground surrounded by the tracks of bighorn sheep. The eagle is silent, and then lifts off with a seven-foot wingspan.

For lunch, I eat salami and chocolate with my feet resting on my skis. The Kaibab ("mountain lying down" in Ute) near the Utah border stretches flat and spiked with trees and there is no sound in the cold forest. In one more day, we will break out of the prison of conifers at Swamp Point and stare silently into a canyon called the Grand.

I am getting tired as the day wears on and my boots march raggedly across a creosote flat that flows toward the Gila River. The Growler Valley spins ahead, thirty-three miles of creosote like a sea of wheat in Kansas. A round stone ball appears by my foot, something centuries old that has been waiting. I stoop and rub my fingers across the smooth granite surface of a prehistoric toy lost before Columbus stepped on board his first ship.

We make camp at 10 p.m. and throw the bags down in a slight clearing of the dune's bramble. Our legs bleed from the fangs of the bramble, and we can still taste the salt air rolling off the Sea of Cortez. All around us the ground is pocked with rat holes, the sand laced with the undulating track of sidewinders. A moon works across the eighteen-mile-wide swath of sand, and I lay among the thorn bushes listening to the night world. A few hours before, my boot went down three inches from a sidewinder, and neither the snake nor I reacted.

A midnight moon washes across the glaciers of Mount Rainier. I lie awake in an alpine meadow and hunger for the big white mountain.

It is 2 a.m. in Big Pass facing the Mohawk Valley and I step on a rattler. The snake slides away to a small brittlebush gleaming in the moonlight. I lie down nearby and dream with my eyes open as the June air washes over me with 100 degree heat. I ache everywhere and want to push on.

At dawn the Catalinas emerge from the darkness as a fist full of peaks and spires. I light the small stove, and sweet cocoa fires up my body in the gray cold of first light. The day stretches before me with possibilities. Perhaps I will fish for trout in the Wisconsin lake nestled in the cutover region. Or watch the desert bighorn graze on the cliffs of Aravaipa Canyon north of the Galiuros. I may take my Newfoundland dog walking in the February snows of the Massachusetts Berkshires and suddenly stumble out of the big maple forest and stand by the almost buried stone wall that circles the small cemetery of dead from the Revolutionary War.

As the light grows, the city sounds of Tucson begin to seep up from the plain now being buried by housing, and I place another kettle of water on to boil. Cathedral and Window peaks look like gods as clouds wipe their stone faces. There are so many places to go. The mountain is so big and spreads out like a pool from the eroding base. The birds begin to break their night-long silence, and my boots hunger to walk the rivers and mountains and plains that spill across the maps stored in my head. That is what a day is like for me when I hike in some canyon that the map insists is limited to a small patch of the Santa Catalina Mountains.

That is a part of me. But another part feeds off the fact that I am a fool for my time and place in the history of this planet. The world is crackling with energy—electrical, nuclear, fossil—and with booze, drugs, and tires screaming around dark curves, and I am drawn to this thunder. I endorse energy conservation, and I am hooked on bouts of long-distance driving—2,000 miles at a crack without stopping for anything but gasoline or slowing for anything but speed traps. For me the highway is a potent drug, and I have no problem with the fact that my country seems centered simply on going, not on getting anywhere in particular, just on the going.

So when I think about what wild ground means to me and why I find it precious, I realize a basic fact. It is not simply threatened by the various bogey men of my time—the capitalists, the zany urban throngs, the flat faces of bureaucrats, the deadened minds of wage slaves, businessmen, greed fiends, hustlers, flim flam artists, bunco men, stockbrokers, real estate developers, lawyers, gangsters, travel agents, and used car salesmen. It is threatened by me.

I am by nature a person suspicious of the economic machine that feeds me. And yet I am a captive of that economic machine, and my mind is structured by its lessons and demands. I consume its wealth with zest. I drive a truck, watch a color television, and write on a computer, but I cannot overcome the feeling that these objects and the industrial culture that produced them are temporary things, a kind of fat beast feeding on the bounty of the earth that will starve to death within the next century, or at least be severely diminished.

Like most strong feelings, this one is grounded in evidence yet almost impervious to reason or argument. It is simply my sense of things and no more metaphysical or fantastic than those offered by proponents of space colonies, cybernetic networks, star wars, and a planet where everyone has a niche in some service industry and apparently no one gets a hand dirty digging the earth or hammering metals into products.

I think places like the Santa Catalinas must be preserved and restored regardless of the future success of machine culture and urban man. Should the future be more of the same—more growth, more products, more people—then natural islands such as the mountain will be even more precious to our descendants as they look up at the peaks from their empire of safe, paved streets. And should this phase we call industrialism fail and become an episode in human history, the natural areas like the mountain will function as treasure houses from which the armies of biological life can surge outward, repopulating and utilizing the sapped and abandoned ground.

In the case of the Catalinas, I can think of no greater future asset for my city than to make the range a complete wilderness. When a million or a million-and-a-half people live within Tucson's confines, the residents will be able to boast that just beyond their jurisdiction lives a wild, free mountain. In a nation where people already must travel long distances to taste the world that greeted their ancestors, Tucson will be able to say such ground exists cheek to jowl with its factories, freeways, and tall office buildings.

The way to save and preserve the mountain is quite simple. We seem to favor notions that hogtie themselves with complications, but this is not such a proposal. We should take to heart Aldo Leopold's challenge and try to think like a mountain. Imagine you are the range, a huge body sprawled under the desert sun. For millions of years, you have lived at a pace and rhythm that human beings can measure but never comprehend. Then in less than a century, new men come and dig big holes in your skin. Exotic beasts called cattle are released and mow down the plants that stand guard over your surface. Thousands and thousands of trees fall and are dragged away so that these invaders can smelt ore gouged from your body. Highways lance deep into your being like long cuts made by a butcher knife. Bulldozers lop off the top of your head, electronic towers punch into your hide, and observatories sprout like warts. Cabins fester among the folds of your skin and pump poisons into the veins of your roaring streams. Cars and trucks race across you and create a demand to cut deeper and more frequently with that butcher knife. Houses and resorts nibble at your extremities, and you hope these wounds do not turn gangrenous and spread rot deeper into your body. And the physicians called in to handle your case, the various government agencies that handle your health-care problems, never speak of a cure for these ailments. In fact, these doctors do not really consult you, but prefer to do business with the forces that have made you sick. They talk of something called multiple use, a way in which all the things now plaguing you can feast in some imagined harmony upon your huge form. With each passing day, your strength dwindles but your attendants do not seem alarmed by this fact. Your chart does not say critical or stable or chronic, but simply, "Land of Many Uses."

I think the doctors should consider some new medicine if we wish for the patient to survive our care.

The paved highway must be removed over time. At present, there is a plan afoot to enlarge the route. This is a mistake. Projected population increases suggest the need for a smaller road not a bigger one. As the human numbers grow, the highway should be scaled back. Hours of use should be gradually diminished, and numbers of cars allowed on the mountain at any one time controlled. The mountain that suffers with a city of half a million people living at its base will be devoured by the proposed city of a million to a million and a half. When the city reaches 1.5 million, the road must be closed and preserved perhaps as a curiosity from an innocent age when no one, not even F. E. A. Kimball and the other highway proponents of the past, could imagine such a crush of numbers.

All-terrain cycle

The cabins should be bought up and leveled. They provide pleasure for very few and pollution for everyone who visits the mountain. No one should live on the mountain. The seventy electronic sites and the observatories should be removed. Relaying messages and investigating the heavens have their value, but it is slight measured against the value of a wild mountain. The land on the backside stretching from Oracle Ridge to Redington Pass and down below to the San Pedro River should be bought and emptied of mines, ranches, and roads. These claims should be paid with their current value set off against the loot such enterprises have already taken from the land. Also, a bill for damages to the mountain by such businesses should be factored into the final price. Soon, this bajada and slope will be the only section left that will suggest the former power of the mountain. It should be preserved as a model of what this place was before the freeways, subdivisions, and millions. Our descendants will be grateful for the opportunity to see a hint of landscape free of the bulldozer's bite.

In short, the mountain over time should be left to itself. People who want to walk in to look around, to hunt, or to explore are welcome. People can go elsewhere who will not travel without a machine or spend the night without a roof over their heads.

It is traditional to damn such proposals as elitist, as ideas that cut off great numbers of humanity from enjoyment of the out-of-doors. It is said that the aged, the infirm, and the handicapped are denied access by such ideas. This is true.

The mountain I have described will not be something like hot water or cold beer, an indulgence instantly available to everyone. To go there will call for more than a tank of gas and a machine. Why is that fact so terrible? Do we want statistics like 1.3 million recreation visitor days per year, or do we want a mountain? It is no longer 1880, and we do not need to flee to the high country to escape summer heat. We do not need to bulldoze a mountain so that we can have a picnic and throw down a six-pack. We can no longer defend slaughtering groves of trees 500 years old so that people can try their luck at skiing in those random years when enough snow comes to the peaks. We hack the mountain down to our size for very trivial reasons, and in doing so we risk losing something that has grown increasingly rare, wild ground that questions the way we live. The only way to make our peace with the mountain is to get off it.

Of course the Catalinas are but a small part of a global assault on the remnant patches of wild ground. I live in a time when the tropical forests are disappearing, the arctic is probed for fossil fuels, and the heart of Africa and South America are consumed by millions of people breeding billions.

Closer to home, we do not have to look far to see the future of urban wildernesses like the Catalinas if we choose to do nothing. The San Gabriel Mountains next to Los Angeles demonstrate to us the content of the coming decades. This range struggles to breathe in clouds of smog and bears the thunder of the enormous urban population driving the roads to picnic and catch a glimpse of a forest.

Usually our response to this ongoing orgy of consumption is indifference. Sometimes we offer up plans as an answer, endless plans that go through years of drafts and revisions and that sputter along promising multiple use and yet seem to lead us toward futures where the ground is sapped of any use at all. While we talk of such matters, we know the deserts are growing, the forests shrinking, and the rate of extinction of species accelerating. If the sky is not yet falling, it is certainly growing dark with the smoke of our machines and factories, and our watersheds slip toward sterility from the acid rain produced as byproducts of our power systems.

I think it is time to face the obvious. We cannot use wild ground without diminishing it. We must leave it wild. The mountain needs friends, guards, advocates, and soldiers. And the work to be done is simple: get the cattle, mines, houses, roads, ski runs, towers, and observatories off the range. We do not need more environmental impact statements. We will always need the mountain.

And we need the mountain all over the country. We must guard the Bradshaws next to Prescott, the Superstitions abutting Phoenix, the front range facing Colorado Springs, Denver, and Boulder, the Mohave Desert at Los Angeles's backdoor, the Cabeza Prieta of southwestern Arizona, the hardwood forests of Appalachia, the swamps of Florida, the big woods of the Upper Midwest, and the great wall of the Cascades and Sierra Nevada. Wherever American people concentrate in cities, wild ground must be set aside, resurrected, and made inviolate. No more roads, trams, picnic tables, timber permits, mines, or grazing rights. No more fantasies of multiple use. These places are fully used by the things living there, and our schemes to chip away a piece here and manage a chunk there rob the life already present.

It is not simply that we must protect some scraps from our future industrial lusts; we must begin to give back, to take out roads, to buy up commercial interests, and to restore islands of life that do not answer to our ways or cash registers. Reconstituting the Santa Catalinas is but a small part of this task. We have taken enough from this continent, more than enough.

I camp in the quiet canyon on the Catalinas' backside. I spend two nights and days doing nothing, nothing at all. Eventually, the whiskey runs out, but this does not matter. I read a book. I sit and stare. I listen and hear nothing but the rush of water and the soft breath of the breeze working through the trees. I make notes and then do not look at them again.

I sense the distance between what I have come to think and what others think. A few months ago, I interviewed Roy Drachman, a man in his late seventies who has spent a lifetime converting the local desert into the boom town of Tucson. He is a great success and spends much of his time at his second home in La Jolla, California. He was born in a barrio near downtown Tucson, and as a leader in the urban renewal campaigns of the 1960s saw his boyhood home bulldozed to make way for a new community center. He felt this demolition spelled progress. He told me as a boy he liked to hike the mountains and the desert. But he thinks things have gone too far, that too much land is locked away by the federal government and the state, and that what we now need is more private land on which to build houses, resorts, shopping centers, factories, cities, towns, and dreams.

He is not alone in these thoughts. The history of land use in this country teaches that as a people we hold the earth to be potential private property to be bought and sold and made use of. I have drifted away from this history and this ambition. I have returned to the swamp.

I did not expect this to happen. I would prefer a country where there were no rules and where the land offered endless promise and unrestrained human beings could work out their own salvation or damnation. I would prefer a country that creaked along with little or no government. When I was a boy, my old man liked to tell me of a shipwrecked Irishman who washed up on an island. People found him half dead on the beach, choking on the sea water in his lungs. He coughed and asked them, "Is there a government?" and when they said yes, he snorted, "I'm against it." I understand that story.

But since I was born, my country has grown by tens of millions of people, and each and every one of these people has shared in the economic boom and greatly increased the amount of material consumed per capita. I was ten years old before my parents bought a fan. The thing entered our apartment like a rare artifact and was proudly placed in a window to struggle against Chicago's torrid, humid summers. Now I live on the ragged edge of the economy and yet my house is stuffed with appliances. This bounty comes from the land, and the land is being used up. I can no longer trust that

Bull snake

The front range

wild ground will survive through some kind of benign neglect. We need rules, rules that toss us out of such places.

When I was a kid in Illinois, my aunt lived in the country and hauled her garbage to a bridge and pitched it into the creek. I can still see the dark coffee grounds and shiny tin cans cascading into the green water. Such an act did not seem to make much difference then. I will never live in a world where I can enjoy my aunt's innocence about the capacity of the land to bear punishment.

I have visited too many mountains. At dawn on the third day, we pack up and climb the slopes to the crest. There is no trail, and we cling to small oaks as we struggle up the sharp incline. We feel very strong now, and the hike out is much easier than the hike in.

When we get to the top, I fire up my diesel pickup, a machine whose day I trust will eventually end with the dwindling of the oil beds, and drive down the paved highway I want ripped out. My life has no tidy consistency. On the way, we pass surveyors plotting the new enlargement of the road and at the base we are greeted by a sign announcing a shopping center that will be built soon.

We stop at a restaurant and eat greedily. Out the window, I can see the mountain looming through a wall of dust and smog. We are dirt-caked, red from the sun, and we stink. The waiter asks if we have been hiking, and we say yes and he seems reassured.

On the wall, Mayo Indian blankets are offered for sale, the work of a tribe far south on the Río Mayo just below Sonora. There seems no end to our desire to own and market little totems of that wild, original world we are busy paving. Everything I thought on the mountain begins to ebb away, ground down by the power of the city and the tenacity of its hungers. I can feel myself being seduced again by the safe, straight streets. Huge machines chew the earth nearby, fashioning an interchange for the growing population of cars and trucks.

Construction in Tucson

The mountain waits, doing nothing, saying nothing. In a valley of words, energies, and schemes, the big range remains mute. It seems almost to have accepted the future. I no longer can.

There is an old Papago song that came out of the salt pilgrimage the tribesmen once made across the Pinacate to the Sea of Cortez, a long walk that functioned within the tribe as a vision quest. The salt trek is no longer made and the songs are now dead, entombed in books fashioned by anthropologists. The Papagos themselves are deeply mired in alcoholism, federal welfare, and the urge to get their piece of modern economic life. Frog Mountain has largely passed from their concern. They are not a people that lend themselves easily to our endless desire in books and movies to fantasize the New World before we sacked it. They do not look particularly noble, and they refrain from wearing feathers or dwelling in quaint prehistoric homes. But the ideas they once put forth in songs interest me because they came from a people who used the land and thought they were tied to the land until the end of time. Consider one song:

> Most wretched lies the earth which you have made,
> The trees which you have planted leafless stand.
> The birds you threw into the air
> Alight in vain and do not sing.
> The springs of water are gone dry.
> The beasts that run upon the earth,
> They make no sound.
> Indeed, indeed, my nephew;
> Is this so hard to change?
> Not hard it is if all think and act with one accord.
> Know this and go back whence you came.

I think it is time to start singing the old songs again.

We finish lunch and go home. Everywhere I look in my town, I see the work going on. Everywhere I look in my town, I see the mountain peeking through the rising forest of girders.

When I first saw Tucson and the mountain, they had a different look. In the winter of my eleventh year, the old man disappeared again and was gone for weeks riding trains back and forth across the country. When he returned from this scout, he gave me a map and announced the family would move to a place called Tucson in the desert Southwest. I unfolded the thing, and the city spread before me as a maze of thin blue lines tracking streets and highways. To the north the lines thinned and then ended. I asked the old man why this void suddenly appeared in the neat grid work of the roads. He said there was a mountain, a big one called the Santa Catalinas.

Snow lay on the ground outside the Chicago apartment, and the clouds hung slate gray. I sprawled on the floor of the living room puzzling out the nature of the thing in the blank space on the map, wondering over a force that could stop a city in its tracks.

Almost three decades have passed since that day and now the maps have a different look. The thin blue lines reach closer to the range and probe its canyons, overwhelm its foothills, and stalk the wild ground on two of its three sides. I am forty, but I am old enough to drive through neighborhoods where I plugged rabbits as a kid and to see houses march across desert where I once struggled to get deer and javelina within my gunsights. The mountain no longer seems like a thing that can stop a city in its tracks; it seems more like a cornered beast. When I hike the Catalinas now and stare down at the valleys, I feel I am on an island, one that is being constantly eroded by the fierce waves of energy sweeping across the desert floor. When I leave the city for the mountain, I walk past bulldozers on my way to the trailhead.

That is one mountain I have come to know, a thing shrinking before my eyes.

And then there is another mountain. A year ago, I decided to walk every trail in the Santa Catalina Mountains. I have not done this, and I may never finish the task. The mileage is not so great—perhaps 200 miles of paths—but the motive for such an act has vanished. The mountain takes more time than I had originally thought. Canyons that look to be an afternoon's work now promise to occupy me for months, years, maybe forever. And there are all the side canyons and hills and peaks without trails and all the streams and springs where a week can vanish without my advancing one foot. I now understand how Buster Bailey could spend a life learning one slab of the range's north side.

I think I have stumbled onto Frog Mountain, that rich ground full of power that lived without a management plan and offered few clues to human beings. I am the product of a world that has gone too far to sprinkle cornmeal to placate Navitcu, and I am incapable of such an action. I am not in the market for new gods. But I have come to understand the value of such a spirit and such an act.

I have found a place where I can learn but not exert control.

The valley is already shackled with the power of my culture. The riverbeds are being scraped, the banks stabilized with chemical compounds, and the meandering courses converted to long, dull, safe tubes for drainage. Each day more of the desert goes under, and new plants and animals move in. Already, the city has more starlings than cactus wrens. I do not look for surprises in my city. It was not built to provide the unexpected but to guarantee that nothing can happen out of the ordinary. Nothing at all.

Frog Mountain has a different will. Here the floods still tear unchecked down canyons and strip them. Here the storms catch one off guard and pound the body with their raw fury. Here there can be total silence on a gray afternoon and then a band of coatis will bound away under the low oaks.

New homes under construction

Underneath the management plans, underneath the development plans, underneath all the detailed maps of this range labeled the Santa Catalinas, Frog Mountain still lives and breathes. The pulse is slowing, the breath comes with increasing difficulty, and the body is scarred and wounded, but the thing is still alive and can be brought back to full vigor.

That is an act worth doing. If Frog Mountain is saved, the city will always have one thing that we cannot create ourselves. A place that mocks the safe limits of our own imagination. A place that does not obey. Frog Mountain.

Along Oracle Highway, north of Tucson

LATE AFTERNOON

You're born to be a thief and killer,
And a general all-around pest,
But I hate to do this pardner
'Cause you're part of our Old West.
You and me are sort of brothers,
With our backs against the wall,
In an act that's nearly over
And the curtains about to fall.

BUSTER BAILEY'S VERSION OF THE LAMENT OF AN
OLD-TIME COWBOY UPON KILLING A COYOTE

The dogs go to ground in the afternoon heat, and Buster Bailey waits out the inferno under his ramada. Big gravel trucks roar by, and the work along the freeway continues. Tucson basks in its best year of growth since 1951; Buster sits among his wrecked cars and trucks more interested in his dogs than this surge of Sunbelt energy.

I have come by to settle accounts. After months of walking around the mountains, I want to hear what he thinks should be done with them. I have this hope that Buster and I will cut through a lot of guff and get down to some level of agreement, a kind of truce between the cowman and the backpacker. This is not likely. I have gotten a haircut and Buster allows as this makes me a little more human looking, but he is still leery of anyone whose idea of a good time consists of walking around the mountains with a fifty-pound pack.

He sits there in a lawn chair rescued from the dump wearing a clean shirt, worn Levi's, and old black boots. He prefers rambling around in his head to considering remedies for what ails for the Santa Catalinas. He has a hard time answering my question, what with all his years crowding in the way. He goes through a denunciation of things that have come between him and the Catalinas, a kind of therapeutic tirade. The state park system has made a hash out of his last ranch, he snorts, the Forest Service has let the trails and waterholes go to hell, and the long-haired backpackers have taken over, he adds, casting a suspicious eye on me. The city? Well the city has polluted its own water and a reckoning is coming. This time it will be the flood again (clouds blacker than the ace of spades) and this time it will be fire (I think the mountains will probably burn off, not even be there).

He relishes his gloomy forecast and seems to brighten as he detects a slide in modern morals. "We're drowning in our own filth, nobody can deny that. . . . When the decency, the morals, and the trust are gone. . . . If we could see ahead, we'd probably kill ourselves."

"So I just don't know what's gonna happen to your mountain," he concludes. "It's just no good anymore."

I sit there wondering what in the hell I have come out here for. Is this the same guy who has spent half a century wandering around the Pusch Ridge country? He limps into his shack to get another metal box full of old photographs. There he is again in his boots, jeans, work shirt, and cowboy hat riding a mare on the mountain, leading pack horses up to the top, standing in his corral with the range a backdrop blocking out the sky. He shuffles the images quickly like a deck of cards he has used in many a game and fires each photo into my hands with a short commentary. A mare stands there, nostrils flaring. "That thing right there that you're looking at has been over every trail and pinnacle up there."

He shows me another horse, a pinto, which looks mutely at the camera.

"You could see your reflection on her black rump she was so pretty."

For a man who savors the past and denounces the future, he seems pretty content with life. One eye is bad but the doctors are going to fix that, he snaps. And his bum leg still bothers him but he's got another appointment in a few weeks to see about some surgery, just as soon as he gets his blood pressure under control. He excuses his zest for life by explaining that he hopes to live to see the coming ruin.

I want to tell him what I have decided should be done about the mountain but I do not. I do not think my wish list of changes will start an argument but rather that it will bring silence. I sense Buster is long past imagining that anything can happen to the peaks but ruin. And he prefers to snarl about the ruin rather than entertain futures that do not smack of the conditions he found in 1927. I want to send the cows home; he wants his ranch back. I want to stop the mining of the peaks; he responds that the mountain is already messed up. I want the place saved for the long hike; he is a horseman. I want the road ripped out; he boasts of all the wrecks he pulled from canyons by the Mount Lemmon highway and tosses me photos of crumpled cars and trucks.

So we drop such talk and dive into the mountain that persists beneath all the houses, roads, and people, the mountain that lives in our minds. He wants to take me to a cave on the backside where at the bottom of a deep chamber the air is always cool and a pool of water lies flat and still. He brags on Buster Spring. "By God, the best damn drinking water you ever swallowed." He once sat under a tree by his namesake waterhole and saw seventeen desert bighorn come in to drink. He smiles at that memory.

He hobbles again into his shack and comes back with his scrapbook of dog clippings. He has a new one and insists I read it, not skim it dammit, but read every word. I glance at the article and it looks to be from the *National Enquirer*. Buster is not squeamish about his sources of information. I read on and learn about this man in Britain who goes into a coma and everyone in his family gathers around him at the hospital where the doctors say he is dying. The family decides his dog must join the bedside vigil because he always loved that dog. They hoist the animal onto a roof just outside the man's room and the dog catches the scent of its master and goes into a mournful howl and then barks.

The man snaps awake at the sound of the animal's cry, begins to speak, and soon recovers. It seems he was brought back from the dead by the right call.

Buster beams at the clipping about how salvation is always possible, how it never seems really to be too late.

"If this is true," he says, "this old world is something else."

The gravel trucks keep rolling past, hauling loads to new construction sites. The mountain peers through a wall of dust and smog at the growing city. The afternoon creeps along full of long, hot hours. Buster has a great view of the mountain from his shack in the junkyard, and the range stretches out slumbering.

Development near Sabino Canyon

AFTERWORD

Our attitude toward wild life reverses the usual assumption that wild life should be conserved in so far as is compatible with economic development. Our conviction is that economic development should proceed only so far as is compatible with the conservation of wild life.

ALDO LEOPOLD

A couple of years after the publication of this book, I was asked to appear at a Forest Service hearing to discuss the merits of expanding a ski development in the Santa Catalina Mountains. Being a true believer in democracy and a child trained on Tom Paine and the Whisky Rebellion, I naturally attended this meeting. A local environmental organization had instigated my invitation under the mistaken notion that I knew the mountain. No one knows the mountain, and no one ever will. That is why I wrote a book about the range and why you read it. But we are all hungry to know a little more of the brooding rock pile we call the Catalinas because we need, to borrow that wonderful phrase of F. Scott Fitzgerald's, something commensurate with our capacity for wonder.

The brute facts of the hearing were simple: the ski development had existed on the mountain for decades, had never been planned, had grown willy-nilly by little increments, and was now considered a given. In short, it typified our policies in the national forests and on all the other ground under our dominion. A couple of hundred people filled the auditorium—most of them waffle-stomping tree-buggers, but there was also a healthy contingent speaking for the life-sustaining powers of decent cognac, the spiritual value of fires in the ski lodge, the necessity of lycra clothing, the biological imperative of fornication in alpine chalets, and the importance of riding boards downhill on snow.

I was ushered up on the stage, where I sat with a SWAT team of Forest Service minions in civilian dress and bereft of their comical hats. The issue at hand was rather simple: whether to cut down some Douglas firs that were older than the European conquest of the Western Hemisphere in order to make yet one more ski run on the mountain. As I chatted with the earnest foresters, it soon became apparent to me that in their eyes the merits of this silvicide were beyond question. I had come armed with a quote by John Steinbeck, one plucked from his sad and yet joyous book, *The Log of the Sea of Cortez*. It was, I hoped, my silver bullet to slay the dragons of federal power. As I sat there bantering with the federal officials (who looked upon me as their long-lost pit bull), I glanced through my arsenal:

Other animals may dig holes to live in; may weave nests or take possession of hollow trees. . . . They make little impression on the world. But the world is furrowed and cut, torn and blasted by man. Its flora has been swept away and changed; its mountains torn down by man; its flat lands littered by the debris of his living. . . .

Physiological man does not require this paraphernalia to exist, but the whole man does. He is the only animal who lives outside of himself, whose drive is in external things—property, houses, money, concepts of power. . . . His house, his automobile are a part of him and a large part of him. This is beautifully demonstrated by a thing doctors know—that when a man loses his possessions a very common result is sexual impotence.

Perhaps, it is all a part of the process of mutation and perhaps the mutation will see us done for. We have made our mark on the world, but we have really done nothing that the trees and creeping plants, ice and erosion, cannot remove in a fairly short time.

I suddenly realized that I had brought insufficient weaponry for the encounter. I was underarmed not because I faced crafty government warriors or savage downhill racers but because I was confronting a mind-set that was such a commonplace that anything I might say would appear at best insane, at worst the product of an illegal smile. I listened to official after official report on the proposed ski run, and they all pretty much said what I expected: the whacking of some big trees would have no effect on the mountain, or if it had any effect, it would be a good one. Though I am not noted as a psychic, I had slyly anticipated this line of reasoning. When it comes to tinkering with the natural world, the defense underlying all proposed changes is simply that they will actually change nothing. It does not matter whether the instruments of our pleasure are chainsaws, dams, highways, toxic waste dumps, or houses. I had had a crash course in this Things Just Get Better and Better syndrome shortly after the publication of this book.

The book's tender and moderate thesis had been to blow up the only paved highway leading into the mountain and then leave the mountain alone to heal. The Forest Service, ever keen for public input, had taken heed of my thoughts and had enlarged the existing highway. They named a new lookout (complete with parking for our machines) Babat Toak, Frog Mountain. In addition to this contribution to the commonweal, the Forest Service in the ensuing years had seen to it that more trees had been cut, visitor usage had increased (can't stop people from coming, I'm told), key wildlife had wavered or declined, and the normal patterns of our vaunted stewardship had continued apace.

Eventually, my turn to speak came, and I will (to use the current namby-pamby usage) share with you what I said on that occasion:

I suspect my ideas here tonight will be dismissed by the Forest Service as simplistic, unrealistic, and some other icks. In fact, I'll save them the time and deliver the critique myself: I'll be told that the increasing numbers of people dictate more intensive use of the ski run area. Well, if numbers are the game, why not level the forest and put in a crack park or a casino?

And surely I'll be told about trade-offs—you give up this and get that. Trade-off has a crazed ring to me. It always sounds like the canyon that has been gutted, the stream polluted, or the tree that has been killed has actually just been traded off and is now happily playing Triple A ball for some team in San Diego.

Then there will be the argument of historic use—a rhetorical device that was a favorite of antebellum slaveholders. You'd think Father Eusebio Kina, S.J., had set up the lodge and was a downhill racer. Actually, the ski development was an idea in the forties and a fact in the fifties, and let's face it, it has turned out to be a less-than-great idea.

And then there will be the charge of elitism—I'm kind of curious how you bring this one into play to defend a downhill ski resort.

I suspect there will be charts, cost-benefit analyses, and a kind of bar tab toting up recreational user days. Where do they file recreational user nights—under wildlife?

Land of Many Uses is the slogan of the Forest Service. But so far as I can see, there is actually only one use: anything goes for one species, human beings. The picnic areas are not for the squirrels. The highway is not for the deer. The radio towers and observatories are not for the birds. The cabins in Summerhaven are not for the benefit of the creek. And the ski runs, ski lift, proposed alpine slide, maintenance building, parking lot, and observation deck (I always thought the Santa Catalina Mountains themselves were a pretty dandy observation deck)—well, none of these things are going to benefit the trees killed to make room for them. When black bears dropped in at the cabin slums of Summerhaven a while back, it became a problem story in the newspapers. What kind of national forest are we running where the existence of black bears is a problem and the existence of a bunch of cabins, ski runs, and a lodge is not?

It's hard for me not to wonder if I'm going a little insane or maybe still having afterflashes from my chemical indulgences in the sixties. When I was a kid my dad told me there would be hard times, but he never warned me I'd be dealing with a Forest Service that wondered whether parking lots, observation decks, and alpine slides were more important than the forest itself. Just why are we here tonight talking about ski runs on a mountain with little snow? Why are we considering expanding a ski resort by cutting down ancient trees in something we call a national forest? Did I miss something? Or should we just rename it the Coronado National Ski Run, or the Coronado National Cabin Center, or the Coronado National Lodge Saloon? Or the Coronado National Highway Department?

The Forest Service has been around a long time, and I'm sure that back in the days of Teddy Roosevelt I would have thought it was a great thing with a great mission. But now I think the agency needs somebody with a little bigger vision, someone who can sense that times are changing, a kind of Gandhi or Crazy Horse. If a bunch of Cold Warriors in the United States and the Soviet Union can change their ways and disarm their missiles and stop laying up kegs of poison gas in the cellar like fine wines, surely the Forest Service can change its concept of mission from being dedicated to the single use of the ground by *Homo sapiens* and start dealing with the things that actually live in the forest. We need true multiple use. A plan for use by the trees, by the spotted owls, the warblers. The black bear. The rocks. Especially the rocks.

We need to begin decommissioning things in the forest, just like we mothball and scuttle warships when peace arrives. Stopping this proposed ski run is a tiny first step, but with practice we can finally learn how to walk without falling on our faces. Little children learn to walk all the time—I've actually seen this happen. Look, I'll leave you with a simple rule that will make all these questions easy: Any proposal for a national forest that means there will be less national forest still standing in the end is a bad idea.

I realize now that, as is often the case in my efforts, I had given in to my besetting sin and was far too moderate that night. In fact, when I finished speaking and sat down to what I might modestly record as thunderous applause, the federal official next to me muttered, "You pandered to the audience." And I courteously replied, "You can bet your ass on that." I now agree with that official: I had pandered to the mob, and the time is past for pandering. The hour is growing late on this ball of dirt we call home, and I vow to cease to be The Panderer and to become The Rude Boy.

When I wrote *Frog Mountain Blues* I believed that if one taught people how to love something, they would become better people and better lovers. I still think this is true. After all, I have seen grown men and women love each other, and it is a very pretty sight. But I now know this goal is not sufficient. In the case of Frog Mountain and our national forests, we must become, alas, celibate lovers. It all goes to the heart of the Forest Service idea of multiple use, a vision that must have been constructed by a pimp, a madam, or some other kind of professional consultant. I'll spell out what this concept really means. The Forest Service hosts orgies, and because it must satisfy diverse appetites in our culture, it plans for all tastes: we have a room for those who like whips, a place for the leather freaks, a venue for those who have fetishes of the foot and whatnot, an arena for those who crave them at an unseemly young age, and so forth. Under the mask of language, we call these depraved habits mining, cattle raising, lumbering, hunting, fishing, and on and on. But just for an instant imagine you are a rock or a tree or a flower or an animal or soil. What does multiple use look like then? Well, it looks like a scheme for allowing *Homo sapiens* to have you in different ways. And when you have been had, it is not likely that you are going to be particularly grateful.

Besides, this ongoing federal orgy is not working. We are now bedeviled by a national debate over the cutting of old-growth forest, a debate that ignores the real point. What is old-growth forest? It is the forest that the Forest Service has never managed. It is the stuff that precedes our presence and our actions. It is natural. And if, after a century of silviculture, multiple use, and brilliant management of the national forests, we are finally coming with sharpened fangs for these shreds of old growth, it means we have failed by every criteria we can imagine. We want the old growth because our policy of cutting trees and then replanting the forests has not worked. If it had, why would we need to murder the old growth, the one part of the forest that owes nothing to our genius? If our management of the forests were sound, why do we have to reintroduce California condors? In fact, if we knew what we were doing in the forests, why are they filled with endangered species? If the Forest Service had been employed by what we call the private sector, it would have been given its pink slip long ago.

The obvious conclusion to this litany of failure is that we do not know what we are doing. Don't feel bad about this fact; no sane man or woman actually thinks he or she can understand an ecosystem, much less run one. I've been told this by foresters, wildlife biologists, and other toilers in the natural world. In fact, to introduce a bright note, there is a quiet revolt going on in our federal agencies. The old timber bulls, who looked at a tree and saw lumber or counted wildlife and babbled about harvesting them, are being replaced by men and women who think of ecosystems as intricate wholes, who are humble about their knowledge, ravenous to learn more, and restrained in their appetites. These new men and women will run our federal lands in the near future, and for that fact we should thank the Lord. However, like my former self, they tend to fall prey to the sin of moderation, and I wish to lead them from this crooked way to the straight and narrow path that winds upward toward salvation. I will be their Chuck the Baptist and briefly sketch a new, modest, and conservative program that will save our immortal souls and possibly some trees, animals, and plants: it is time, at the very least, to leave our national forests alone. Zero cutting for a generation or two or three. No more damn roads. Good-bye to the cows. Forget mining. Kiss *adiós* to the 4 x 4s, dirt bikes, Skidoos, and other hellcats. And if we need to commune with nature with our backpacks, binoculars, and rifles, why don't we create more nature instead of sacking what little has survived our tender mercies? If this creates unemployment, so be it. When a war ends, the soldiers have to find some other form of fun. The war against our forests must cease, and we must seek other ways of living our lives. Genocide, though a nifty blood sport, never promises a future. After all, the Romans eventually learned how to get through the day without feeding a few Christians to the lions. I'm sure that at first they missed the chomping of jaws, the blood running down the tawny chins, the tongues lapping, and the screams of horror, but they eventually detoxed from their thrills.

Frog Mountain is but a little fragment of our failure, and this failure is now a sin because we actually know better. Frog Mountain can be a little fragment of our penance and perhaps in time our new virtue. We are living in a time of global destruction, and we all know it. We all shrug and say, What can be done? It's too big for anyone to deal with. Well, I'll tell you what can be done. We will right this catastrophe one mountain at a time, one canyon at a time, one hill at a time. And we can begin with the Frog Mountains just outside all our doors, sierras that stare down at our actions in disbelief. We will cease to be moderate. We will say, "Nunca más. Never again." We will become conservative, and like all good conservatives, we will conserve. Every day at sundown we will make sure that we have added a little bit more life to the planet. We will literally expand the earth by letting other living things have a piece of it. And if we do this, our hearts will sing, our sleep will be dreamless and full of joy. At the dawn our bodies will quicken, and Frog Mountain and her numerous global kin will look down upon us and no longer shudder.

Don't tell me this is impossible. I'll tell you what is really impossible: that we can continue to live and act the way we have in the past. Believe me, the problem is not that some spotted owl will perish or that ancient trees will die. The problem is that we will start dying in a big and clumsy way. We have already, I suspect, lost our souls. Next we will lose our lives. I'm an optimist. I believe our souls can be beckoned back and will once again inhabit our bodies. I keep a candle burning every day and every night of the year. I believe we can actually learn to live and let live. In fact, I know it. A bird told me so.

A person's life purpose is nothing more than to rediscover, through detours of art, or love, or passionate work, those one or two images in the presence of which his heart first opened.

Albert Camus

I am by heritage half German. This is not a problem for me so long as I avoid the cooking, although I do have a weakness for parsnips, sauerkraut, and blutwurst. But long before I could ever scribble this page I vowed one very simple thing: I would never be a "good German," closing my eyes to the destruction. Never. I will always know the darkness on the edge of town, I will not deny this knowledge, and I will act on this knowledge or the gods may damn me to all their hells with my consent.

There is another matter I would like to dispatch swiftly: don't ask me what's in it for you. We have been seduced by the bogus notion that self-interest is the only interesting thing, an idea that every faith denounces and mocks. You are going to die, I am going to die, and everything on the mountain is going to die. I don't know the master plan; they will not tell me. But I am certain that if we ask what's in it for us, we will never understand the answer when we are told. Not even if the message comes in words of one syllable, not even if the message comes in the fist of a storm or in the song of a stream.

It is time for you and me to set aside our childish ways. We have some years on us now, and all *Homo sapiens*, it is said, become conservative with time. So let's all get out of the closet and show the world what the conscience of a conservative really looks like. It will be painful standing suddenly in the glare of the sun, but it will be a new and beautiful sight. We will like it. And for the first time in a long time, we will be liked. Perhaps even loved.

Charles Bowden, 1994

They call it paradise
I don't know why.
You call someplace paradise,
Kiss it goodbye.

THE EAGLES, "THE LAST RESORT"

ACKNOWLEDGMENTS

The following people have helped me a great deal in my effort to learn about the Santa Catalinas: Buster Bailey, Gerry Brinkley, David Brown, Neil Carmony, Julian Hayden, Bill Lewis, Tony Zimmerman, and the staff of the Coronado National Forest Service (particularly those at the Catalina station). I want to thank them for their time and kindness.

I also want to thank the staff at the University of Arizona and Arizona Historical Society (particularly Tracy Row). Anne Denny, reference librarian at the Tucson Public Library, was invaluable in helping me ferret out nineteenth-century articles about the range. Certain insights into mountains were given me by B. G. Pyrenees, a student of such matters.

Various drafts of this book were read by Kathleen Dannreuther, Nedra Kayner, Bill Bent, Bill Broyles, Edward Abbey, Dave Brown, Sally Antrobus, and Neil Carmony. I am grateful for their comments.

C.B.

To Ralph Frost and Chuck Scott, whose leadership focused my photojournalist's eye.

To Tim and Lin Caravello, who introduced me to the Santa Catalina Mountains.

To Pete Cowgill, who hiked me into shape while sharing the wild backcountry at Tucson's doorstep.

To *Arizona Highways* magazine for supporting my work during my transition into landscape photography.

Finally, to my wife Margaret for her support and love during some difficult times.

Thanks.

J.D.

BIBLIOGRAPHY

Anyone considering a trip into the Santa Catalina Mountains should take along one book: Pete Cowgill and Eber Glendening's *Trail Guide to the Santa Catalina Mountains* (Rainbow Expeditions, 915 Sherwood Village, Tucson, Arizona, 85710, 1977), written by two men who know and love the mountain. This book and their example have gotten legions of hopeless types, such as myself, out of the house and back onto the land where we belong.

A second book, Ann E. Harrison's, *The Santa Catalinas: A Description and History*, has proven a godsend in writing this book. Unfortunately, the text exists only in typescript (available in Special Collections, The University of Arizona Library) and represents an unfinished history written by Harrison for the Forest Service in the early 1970s. The manuscript is based on numerous interviews and historical sources.

What follows are some of the materials I have used in this book. The list is by no means exhaustive of the possible sources pertinent to the Santa Catalinas. I have not written a history of the range and much rich material remains hidden in the archives (for example, the brief essays of the late Glenton Sykes) or locked in the memories of people still alive. Ted Knipe's index to the *Arizona Daily Star*, 1879–1909 (in the archives of the Arizona Historical Society, Tucson) suggests the wealth of detail still buried in the old records.

Ames, Charles R. "A History of the Forest Service." *The Smoke Signal* 16 (Fall 1967).

Anonymous. "Arizona as a Hunting Ground" [Catalinas full of game especially wild turkeys]. *Forest and Stream* 28 (April 6, 1882): 185.

———. "The Fauna of Arizona." *Mining and Scientific Press* 46 (March 3, 1883): 146.

Bandelier, Adolph Francis Alphonse. "Southwestern Fine Timber." *Nation* 43 (July 1886): 8.

Brown, David E. *Arizona's Tree Squirrels*. Phoenix: Arizona Game and Fish Department, 1984.

———, ed. "Biotic Communities of the American Southwest—United States and Mexico." *Desert Plants* 4, nos. 1–4 (1982).

———. *The Grizzly in the Southwest*. Norman: University of Oklahoma Press, 1985.

———. *The Wolf in the Southwest: The Making of an Endangered Species*. Tucson: The University of Arizona Press, 1983.

Brown, Herbert. "The Scarlet Ibis." *Auk* 16 (July 1899): 270.

———. "Stone Squares in Arizona." *American Antiquarian* 21 (May 1899): 184.

Cockrum, E. Lendell. *Mammals of the Southwest*. Tucson: The University of Arizona Press, 1982.

Cowgill, Pete, and Eber Glendening. *Trail Guide to the Santa Catalina Mountains*. Tucson: Rainbow Expeditions, 1977.

Crosswhite, Frank S. "'J. G. Lemmon & Wife,' Plant Explorers in Arizona, California, and Nevada." In *Desert Plants* 1, no. 1 (August 1979): 12–21.

Dodge, E. S. "Letter from E. S. Dodge" [on shooting an antelope at Acadia ranch, Oracle, Arizona, on Catalinas north side]. *Recreation* 11 (October 1898): 307.

Doutt, J. Kenneth. *A Field Note "Diary" of a Scientific Collecting Trip to Arizona in 1927* [a record of a field trip to the Santa Catalina and Santa Rita mountains].Typescript.

Flader, Susan L., ed. *The Great Lakes Forest: An Environmental and Social History*. Minneapolis: The University of Minnesota Press, 1983.

Flader, Susan L. *Thinking Like a Mountain: Aldo Leopold and the Evolution of an Ecological Attitude Toward Deer, Wolves and Forests*. Columbia: University of Missouri Press, 1974.

Goodwin, Grenville. *The Social Organization of the Western Apache*. Chicago: University of Chicago Press, 1942.

———. *Western Apache Raiding and Warfare*. Edited by Keith H. Basso. Tucson: The University of Arizona, 1971.

Gustafson, A. M., ed. *John Spring's Arizona*. Tucson: The University of Arizona Press, 1966.

Harrison, Anne E. *The Santa Catalinas: A Description and History*. Typescript. Tucson: The University of Arizona Special Collections.

Hinton, Leanne, and Lucille J. Watahomiche, eds. *Spirit Mountain: An Anthology of Yuman Story and Song*. Tucson: The University of Arizona Press, 1984.

Hornaday, William T. *Camp-Fires on Desert and Lava*. Tucson: The University of Arizona Press, 1983 [1908].

Lee, Katy. *Ten Thousand Goddamn Cattle: A History of the American Cowboy in Song, Story, and Verse*. Flagstaff: Northland Press, 1976.

Leopold, Aldo. *A Sand County Almanac*. New York: Ballantine Books, 1978 [1949, 1953].

Lowe, Charles H. *Arizona's Natural Environments*. Tucson: The University of Arizona Press, 1964.

Lurnholtz, Carl. *New Trails in Mexico*. Glorieta, New Mexico: Rio Grande Press, 1971 [1912].

Monson, Gale, and Lowell Sumner, eds., *The Desert Bighorn: Its Life History, Ecology, and Management*. Tucson: The University of Arizona Press, 1980.

Polzer, Charles W., S. J. "Legends of Lost Missions and Mines." *The Smoke Signal* 18 (Fall 1968).

Rhoads, Samuel N. "A Visit to Arizona by a Traveling Ornithologist." *Friend 45* (7th day, 8th month, 1891): 34–35; (7th day, 9th month, 1891): 41–43.

Russell, Don. *The Lives and Legends of Buffalo Bill*. Norman: University of Oklahoma Press, 1960.

Scott, William Earl Dodge. "Early Spring Notes from the Mountains of Southern Arizona." *Auk 2* (October 1885): 348–56.

———. "On the Breeding Habits of Some Arizona Birds" [bird life on the San Pedro Slopes of the Catalinas]. *Auk 2* (January 1885): 1–7; (April 1885): 159–65; (July 1885): 242–46; (October 1885): 321–26; (January 1886): 81–86.

———. "Winter Mountain Notes from Southern Arizona." *Auk 2* (April 1885): 172–74.

Shreve, Forrest. *The Vegetation of a Desert Mountain Range as Conditioned by Climatic Factors*. Washington, D.C.: The Carnegie Institution of Washington, 1915.

Sonnichsen, C. L. *Tucson: The Life and Times of an American City*. Norman: The University of Oklahoma Press, 1982.

Wagoner, J. J. *History of the Cattle Industry in Southern Arizona, 1540–1940*. University of Arizona Social Science Bulletin, vol. 20, pp. 1–132.

Whitakker, R. H., and W. A. Niering. "Vegetation of the Santa Catalina Mountains, Arizona: I. Ecological Classification and Distribution of Species." *Journal of the Arizona Academy of Science 3*, no. 1 (March 1964): 9–34.

———. "Vegetation of the Santa Catalina Mountains, Arizona: A Gradient Analysis of the South Slope." *Ecology 46*, no. 4 (Early Summer, 1965): 429–52.

ABOUT THE AUTHOR

Throughout his thirty-four nonfiction books and his work for *GQ*, *Harper's*, *Esquire*, and *Mother Jones*, as well as newspapers, CHARLES BOWDEN'S main focus was the desert borderlands of the Southwest. He wrote eloquently about all the key issues—drug-related violence, illegal immigration, and the environment. Bowden was a Pulitzer Prize nominee, and his books include *Blue Desert*, *Blood Orchid*, *Killing the Hidden Waters*, *Some of the Dead Are Still Breathing*, *The Sonoran Desert*, and *Blues for Cannibals*. Winner of the 1996 Lannan Literary Award for Nonfiction, he spent most of his life in Arizona, exploring the mountains and the desert he loved. He died in 2014.

ABOUT THE PHOTOGRAPHER

Pulitzer Prize–winning photographer JACK W. DYKINGA blends fine art photography with documentary photojournalism. He is a regular contributor to *Arizona Highways* and *National Geographic* and is the author or photographer of numerous books, most recently *A Photographer's Life.*

"A beautifully written, handsomely illustrated love poem to a mountain range that has the fatal curse of being not merely too awesome in its beauty for its own good but, worse, too accessible to man."

—*Los Angeles Times Book Review*

"[Bowden's] prose trembles with a raw and vital energy. . . . *Frog Mountain Blues* is part bitterness, part lament, a love story and a tragedy."

—*New York Times Book Review*

"[*Frog Mountain Blues*] delineates the creeping environmental degradation that occurs when a boomtown pushes toward a wilderness. . . . [Bowden's] narrative is admirably supported by Dykinga's dramatic photographs."

—*Publishers Weekly*

"A personal and provocative work . . . [that] makes an attractive—and effective—plea for wilderness preservation."

—*Washington Post*

Charles Bowden (1945–2014) was the author of many acclaimed books about the American Southwest and U.S.-Mexico border issues. He was a contributing editor for *GQ*, *Harper's*, *Esquire*, and *Mother Jones*. His honors include a PEN First Amendment Award and a Lannan Literary Award for Nonfiction.

Cover design by Leigh McDonald
Cover photo by Keith Marroquin

THE UNIVERSITY OF ARIZONA PRESS

Tucson, Arizona 85721
www.uapress.arizona.edu

ISBN 978-0-8165-3792-1

9 780816 537921